VOICES FROM ARIEL:
Ten-Minute Plays Reflecting the Jewish Experience

A Collection of Ten Short Plays

Compiled and Edited by
JULIANNE BERNSTEIN
and
DEBORAH BAER MOZES

Dramatic Publishing
Woodstock, Illinois • London, England • Melbourne, Australia

*** NOTICE ***

The amateur and stock acting rights to this work are controlled exclusively by THE DRAMATIC PUBLISHING COMPANY without whose permission in writing no performance of it may be given. Royalty fees are given in our current catalog and are subject to change without notice. Royalty must be paid every time a play is performed whether or not it is presented for profit and whether or not admission is charged. A play is performed any time it is acted before an audience. All inquiries concerning amateur and stock rights should be addressed to:

DRAMATIC PUBLISHING
P. O. Box 129, Woodstock, Illinois 60098

COPYRIGHT LAW GIVES THE AUTHOR OR THE AUTHOR'S AGENT *THE EXCLUSIVE RIGHT TO MAKE COPIES.* This law provides authors with a fair return for their creative efforts. Authors earn their living from the royalties they receive from book sales and from the performance of their work. Conscientious observance of copyright law is not only ethical, it encourages authors to continue their creative work. This work is fully protected by copyright. No alterations, deletions or substitutions may be made in the work without the prior written consent of the publisher. No part of this work may be reproduced or transmitted in any form or by any means, electronic or mechanical, including photocopy, recording, videotape, film, or any information storage and retrieval system, without permission in writing from the publisher. It may not be performed either by professionals or amateurs without payment of royalty. All rights, including but not limited to the professional, motion picture, radio, television, videotape, foreign language, tabloid, recitation, lecturing, publication, and reading are reserved.

For performance of any songs and recordings mentioned in this play which are in copyright, the permission of the copyright owners must be obtained or other songs and recordings in the public domain substituted.

©MCMXCIX by
JULIANNE BERNSTEIN, HINDI BROOKS, LOU GREENSTEIN,
LESLIE B. GOLDSTEIN, DANIEL BRENNER, MICHAEL ELKIN,
and VIVIAN GREEN

Printed in the United States of America
All Rights Reserved
(VOICES FROM ARIEL:
Ten-Minute Plays Reflecting the Jewish Experience)

ISBN 0-87129-895-3

IMPORTANT BILLING AND CREDIT REQUIREMENTS

All producers of the play *must* give credit to the author(s) of the play in all programs distributed in connection with performances of the play and in all instances in which the title of the play appears for purposes of advertising, publicizing or otherwise exploiting the play and/or a production. The name of the author(s) *must* also appear on a separate line, on which no other name appears, immediately following the title, and *must* appear in size of type not less than fifty percent the size of the title type. Biographical information on the author(s), if included in this book, may be used on all programs. *On all programs this notice must appear:*

"Produced by special arrangement with
THE DRAMATIC PUBLISHING COMPANY of Woodstock, Illinois"

VOICES FROM ARIEL:
Ten-Minute Plays
Reflecting the Jewish Experience

A Collection of Ten Short Plays
For up to 17 actors (7 men and 10 women)
(Each play has 1 to 3 characters)

Contents

Introduction..................................... vii
Production History ix

Section I: Reflections on 20th-Century Jewish Life
'Til Death Do Us Plots by Julianne Bernstein........... 3
Class Act by Michael Elkin 10
Where's Your Stuff? by Daniel Brenner.............. 19
The Foot Peddler by Vivian Green 26
Smoke by Louis Greenstein 34

Section II: A Minyan of Women
Single Jewish Female by Julianne Bernstein.......... 43
In Spite of Everything by Hindi Brooks.............. 55
The Ger (The Convert) by Leslie B. Gold
and Louis Greenstein 63

Section III: White Spaces Black Letters
A Golden Opportunity by Julianne Bernstein 73
Interview with a Scapegoat by Louis Greenstein 83

About the Authors................................ 93

Theatre Ariel is dedicated to illuminating the rich social, cultural, and spiritual heritage of the Jewish people. It believes that Jewish theatre strengthens Jewish identity while also serving as a bridge between people of all cultures, breaking down myths and silent fears that keep us apart. Theatre Ariel produces and commissions work that serves as a prism through which we can view the American Jewish experience. Our writers also create theatre that draws its inspiration from ancient stories, bringing contemporary insight to sacred texts: reflecting on the past, examining the present and envisioning the future.

Theatre Ariel wishes to thank their funders: Pennsylvania Council on the Arts, Philadelphia Cultural Fund, Stewart Huston Charitable Trust, Joulson Foundation, Joseph Stein Foundation, Lawrence E. Hirsch, Juliet I. Spitzer and Philip Wachs.

Introduction

It was not long after founding Theatre Ariel in 1990 that I discovered how beautifully the 10-minute play genre served our mission and quest for new writers. While 10-minute plays provide the same dramatic structural challenges as do full-length plays, they also exercise the skill of brevity, suggested by the Bard as the "soul of wit." By establishing a Jewish 10-minute play festival, I could discover and encourage emerging writers, while challenging established ones. Though 10-minute play festivals abound, Theatre Ariel created the first festival devoted to exploring the Jewish experience. These festivals successfully expanded the popular notion of "Jewish theatre," all too often confined to just three points in time: the immigrant experience, the Holocaust, and the aging Jew.

In Judaism, it takes 10 adults to make a minyan—a prayer quorum, and just as the 10 members come together to hear the words of the Bible, so does the audience come to experience the words of the playwright. Thus, were all festivals called "Ten by Ten..." joining all 10 plays under a single theme. The plays coming out of our first festival "10X10: Reflections on 20th-Century Jewish Life," take us on a journey into the lives of contemporary American Jews as they grapple with personal and spiritual issues relevant to all people. *Smoke, The Foot Peddler, Class Act, Where's Your Stuff?* and *'Til Death Do Us Plots* create a rich tapestry of contemporary American Jewish experiences including the nostalgic tale of a Pennsylvania working man, the bittersweet saga of being alone after a life partner is gone, a vaudevillian encounter between a father-to-be and the cantor of bar mitzvah pasts, and an engagingly quirky piece about divorce and the afterlife. For our next festival, "10X10: A Minyan of Women," we chose to present the voice of the Jewish woman, a voice all too often neglected in dramatic literature and unheard in spiritual western traditions. I discovered that just as I was searching for viable scripts, so too were these women "searching" for spiritual community in *The Ger*; peace of mind and soul in *In Spite of Everything*; and for a husband in *Single Jewish Female*. Finally, for our third festival, "10X10: White

Spaces Black Letters," we chose to go back to the beginning of Judeo-Christian civilization: the Bible. We commissioned 10 writers to take a section from the Torah, and through creative excavation, find a contemporary vision for these ancient characters and stories. You will laugh out loud at the representation of these two biblical creatures in *An Interview With a Scapegoat* and *A Golden Opportunity*.

Voices From Ariel can be performed as a full evening or as separate scenes by acting duos and trios. If you are an acting teacher, these plays are wonderful for studio classes. As I discovered in my own classes at the Walnut Street Theatre School, the 10-minute play gives students the chance to tackle a complete work. For audiences, one of the great payoffs of these festivals is how they generate and renew interest in new plays. Finally, what you will discover, as have audiences in Philadelphia, Salt Lake City, Atlanta, Jerusalem and Tel Aviv, is that while the characters in these plays are Jewish, the themes are universal and relevant to people of all faiths and cultures.

Finally, I want to thank all the playwrights, directors, designers and actors whose talents brought to life these works and all of the 10-minute plays Theatre Ariel has produced. Our Ten by Ten festivals would not have come to fruition were it not for our funders and the countless individuals who supported them. I especially want to thank my co-editor Julianne Bernstein for all her hard work, dedication and buoyant spirit. Lastly, I want to express my great appreciation to my husband David and daughter Marta for their patience and good humor without which there would be no Theatre Ariel.

Shalom and enjoy!

Deborah Baer Mozes
Artistic Director
Theatre Ariel

10X10: REFLECTIONS ON 20TH-CENTURY JEWISH LIFE
January 20 – February 14, 1993
Annenberg Studio Theatre, Philadelphia, Pa.

Stage Manager .... MARGUERITE PRICE
Set and Properties Design................. BART HEALY
Sound Design .... MARGOT STEIN AZEN
Costume Design .... JOAN SOMMERS
Lighting Design .... ROBERT GUGIELMATTI

'Til Death Do Us Plots
by Julianne Bernstein
Directed by Harold Ellison

Sarah .... BREE SHARP
Lucille .... LESLIE B. GOLD
Art .... JACK HOFFMAN

Class Act
by Michael Elkin
Directed by Deborah Baer Mozes

Sara .... LESLIE B. GOLD

Where's Your Stuff?
by Daniel Brenner
Directed by Deborah Baer Mozes

Ben .... JACK HOFFMAN
Jennifer .... LESLIE B. GOLD
Cantor .... BRUCE KATLIN

The Foot Peddler
by Vivian Green
Directed by Drucie McDaniel

Tom .... JACK HOFFMAN

Smoke
by Louis Greenstein
Directed by Deborah Baer Mozes

Man................................ BRUCE KATLIN

* * * *

10X10: A MINYAN OF WOMEN
February 9 – February 27, 1994
Studio Theater, Walnut Street Theater, Philadelphia, Pa.

Original Music. MARGOT STEIN AZEN, GEELA RAYZEL RAPHAEL
Set and Properties Design................. BART HEALY
Costume Design .... JOAN SOMMERS
Sound Design . MARGOT STEIN AZEN, GEELA RAYZEL RAPHAEL
Lighting Design .... CAROLYN DASCHER

Single Jewish Female
by Julianne Bernstein
Directed by Susan F. Lodish

Teddy........................ GLORIA SALMANSOHN
Leon................................. RAY VERNA
Missie .... RIVI DIAMOND

The Ger (The Convert)
by Leslie B. Gold and Louis Greenstein
Directed by Michele Coleman

Sarah .... SUSANNE CASE
Rabbi................................ RAY VERNA
Mother........................... SELMA DUBROW

In Spite of Everything
by Hindi Brooks
Directed by Deborah Block

Ima .... GLORIA SALMANSOHN
Khana .... ADRIENNE MARTA

* * * *

10X10: WHITE SPACES BLACK LETTERS
May 29 – June 16, 1996
Studio Theater, Walnut Street Theater, Philadelphia, Pa.

Original Music .... JULIET IRENE SPITZER
Set Design.......................... MARK COFTA
Costume Design .... ARIYELA WALD-COHAIN
Lighting Design .... STEPHEN KEEVER
Stage Manager .... ROBERT SCHILLER

A Golden Opportunity
by Julianne Bernstein
Directed by Deborah Block

Calf .... KAREN GETZ
Pica .... BILL BUDDENDORF
Aaron............................... RAY VERNA

"A Golden Opportunity" appeared in the Twentieth Annual Off-Off-Broadway Original Short Play Festival in New York.

Interview with a Scapegoat
by Louis Greenstein
Directed by Deborah Block

Interviewer .... COURTNEY CUSTER
Goat................................. RAY VERNA

Section I:
Reflections on 20th-Century Jewish Life

'TIL DEATH DO US PLOTS
by Julianne Bernstein

CHARACTERS:

SARAH: 13
ART: 40s
LUCILLE: 40s

AT RISE: *Lights up on a tombstone. SARAH holds a prayer book and stands solemnly by her parents. ART and LUCILLE lie side by side in a double casket. They are risen to an angle—so to be seen by the audience.*

SARAH. Mama?
LUCILLE *(opening her eyes)*. Sarah?
SARAH *(with a lump in her throat)*. Oh, Mama. Papa.
ART *(waking up)*. Huh? What the—
LUCILLE *(to ART)*. Shh. *(Pause.)* Sarah? Daddy's not here. He's at his house. Honey, what is it?
SARAH. I love you, Mama. Papa. *(ART is about to say something. LUCILLE silences him.)*
LUCILLE. I love you, too. Are you all right? What do you want?
SARAH. I'll be fine, Mama. Don't worry about me.
LUCILLE. G'night, sweetie. I love you.
SARAH. Good night, Mama. Papa. Sleep well. I love you.
LUCILLE. I love you, too. Go back to sleep, darling. *(Lights dim on SARAH.)* Sarah? *(Pause.)* Sarah?
ART. I should've said something.

LUCILLE. You're not supposed to be here, idiot. You don't belong in this room *or* in this bed. You got no right to be here.

ART. You were just as curious as me, baby.

LUCILLE. I waited three years to sign on the dotted line and get you out of my hair. This little hey-hey means nothing.

ART. Then why'd we do it, huh?

LUCILLE. I don't know. *(Pause.)* Listen, go home and get your slippers outta here.

ART. My slippers?

LUCILLE. They're under the television in the den.

ART. Lucille, I been busting my ass removing myself from this house and you're complaining about a goddamn pair of slippers!

LUCILLE. Shhh. Listen. *(SARAH is reciting the Mourner's Prayer.)* Oh, how'd she learn to say Kaddish so beautiful?

ART. What do you think all that Hebrew school tuition was for?

LUCILLE *(pause)*. *OY GVALT!!!*

ART. No. We're not... are we?

LUCILLE *(panic-stricken)*. Let's go back. We were done with the lawyers at four...

ART. ... we drove away...

LUCILLE. ... in separate cars...

ART. ... mine wouldn't start... the battery, it was...

LUCILLE. ... we looked around for a new one...

ART. I saw a sign...

LUCILLE. Not "BATTERIES." It said "BATH AND TOILET SUPPLIES."

ART. "BATTERIES," it said.

Section I: Reflections on 20-Century Jewish Life

LUCILLE. No. "BATH."
ART. "BATTERIES." And how come you passed on a two-lane?
LUCILLE. You told me to hurry!
ART. The truck. Didn't you see the—?!!
LUCILLE. YOU WARNED ME TOO LATE!! *(Silence.)* We're dead.
ART. You mean...
LUCILLE. We hit a truck and died.
ART. How do you know?
LUCILLE. Women know these things.
ART. Jesus.
LUCILLE *(pause)*. Wait a goddamn minute! What are we doing in a double casket? Who's responsible for this?
ART. Relax.
LUCILLE. I gotta lay by your side forever and you're telling me to relax?
ART. I couldn't pass it up. It was a great deal.
LUCILLE. You should've consulted with me.
ART. Had to move quick or the price was gonna go up.
LUCILLE. Ach! Forget it. I'll handle this myself. Rationally. Logically. *(Pause.)* HELP! SOMEBODY! GET ME OUT OF HERE! HELP!
ART. Get real, Lucille. A deal's a deal.
LUCILLE. A double plot. Thanks a lot. I can't believe you!
ART. I didn't see you taking heed for our future.
LUCILLE. I divorced you. That was my heed. Move over. It's so damn cramped in here.
ART. Remember Flatbush? Remember the twin we slept on when we first got—
LUCILLE. Don't get nostalgic with me. I want my own plot. I want a separate plot.

ART. Well—we can't always get what we want now—can we?

LUCILLE. Ok, schmuck. Here are the rules...

ART. What rules?

LUCILLE. If we're stuck like this—we gotta have rules.

ART. We're not married anymore, I don't have to listen to you—

LUCILLE. Rule number one: No talking allowed.

ART. Forever?

LUCILLE. At least.

ART. That's crazy.

LUCILLE. Rule number two.

ART. Hold it. I got a problem with rule number one.

LUCILLE. What's the problem? Shut your trap.

ART. It's not the rule. It's you makin' up the rule. Acting like Queen Esther.

LUCILLE. Listen and listen good. Because I'm not talking to you or listening to you after this. This was not a good idea. You made a mistake. You blew it.

ART *(pause)*. I think we should make the best of it.

LUCILLE. I think we should both roll over. *(She does so.)*

ART. Come on, Lucille.

LUCILLE. One last time: Don't talk to me. Don't even look at me.

ART. You are so lovely when you're dead.

LUCILLE. That's it! I want to get out of here! I want to switch! I want to lay with somebody else!

ART. Aha!

LUCILLE. What?!!

ART. We're one day dead and you want to hop into bed with somebody else.

LUCILLE. Oh, look who's talking.

Section I: Reflections on 20-Century Jewish Life

ART. I know, Lucille. I know what it must've looked like, but—
LUCILLE. You looked like a jerk.
ART. What?!!
LUCILLE. A fool.
ART. What?!!
LUCILLE. It wasn't you, Art. It just wasn't you.
ART. What are you talking about?
LUCILLE. You looked like a jerk fooling around with another woman. A foolish jerk!
ART. Hey! Are you sayin' I don't have it in me? That I can't...
LUCILLE. You're not the type. You're too straight and narrow.
ART. I don't know what you're talking about.
LUCILLE. You're not the cheatin' type.
ART. Hey, I can cheat just like the rest of 'em.
LUCILLE. That's very good, Art. The YMHA should honor you.
ART *(pause)*. Lucille, are we really dead?
LUCILLE. I told you. We were killed instantly in the Firebird.
ART. I mean—you and me. You think we got a chance?
LUCILLE. No way.
ART. I love you.
LUCILLE. Too late.
ART. Lucille, before I screwed up. Were you happy?
LUCILLE. Don't.
ART. What?
LUCILLE. You're trying to get me to remember all the good times and the *nachas**.

---
* Translation: happiness

8 VOICES FROM ARIEL

ART. Please, Lucille. I'm sorry. I don't know why I did it. I was depressed. I had no life.

LUCILLE. You had me and Sarah.

ART. Please. Forgive me. I got nothing to live for.

LUCILLE. I'm dead. What good's my mercy?

ART. You're my wife.

LUCILLE. Ex-wife.

ART. For heaven's sake, we made love.

LUCILLE. We died. I mean—we made love. I don't know. Did we or didn't we?

ART. Lucille. I broke it off with the *shiksa**. It's over.

LUCILLE. Too late, now.

ART. I promise I'll be good...

LUCILLE. It don't matter now.

ART. I re-pledge my love, my life...

LUCILLE. It's no good anymore.

ART. What? What else can I say?

LUCILLE. Nothing! Nothing!

ART. What the hell do you want from me? What the hell did I take from you that was so precious I can't give it back? Huh?!!

LUCILLE. MY DIGNITY, YOU SON OF A BITCH! MY DIGNITY! THAT'S WHAT YOU TOOK FROM ME! MY GODDAMN DIGNITY! THAT'S WHAT YOU TOOK!!! *(Silence.)*

ART. We're divorced. We're dead.

LUCILLE. Yep. The American Dream.

ART. I should've checked with you first. About the casket, I mean.

LUCILLE. Art? Did you...?

ART. It was an accident, I swear.

* Translation: non-Jewish girl

LUCILLE. Yeah. I know.
ART. I wouldn't take you away from her. Sarah needs you. *(ART yawns.)*
LUCILLE. Go to sleep, Art.
ART. I can't keep my eyes open.
LUCILLE. You had a big day today.
ART. I'll go and try to find a single or something by myself. You can have the double. I bought it for you, I mean.
LUCILLE. Close your eyes, Art. *(He does so and crosses his arms over his chest; SARAH resumes Kaddish.)* Art, wake up.
ART. What?
LUCILLE *(smiling)*. Listen. *(ART listens and smiles as well; but he still cannot keep his eyes open. As LUCILLE listens to SARAH pray, she strokes ART's balding head, unfolds his arms and then continues to stroke him until his body relaxes and he lays his head upon her breast.)*

END

CLASS ACT
by Michael Elkin

CHARACTERS:

SARA: A vivacious 70-year-old bubba.

SETTING: *A school registration booth in a big city. The present.*

AT RISE: *SARA is examining an unseen schedule posted on a wall, squinting and trying to make sense of it. Attired in a Grateful Dead T-shirt, snow-white running shoes that have never seen a gravel road, and baggy shorts, she is a jigsaw puzzle of images from the '20s and '90s.*

SARA (*to unseen registrar*)

Does that say two o'clock...excuse me, miss, does that say, Tuesday, two o'clock?
(Ponders the response.)
You only have volleyball Tuesday at two?
(Grimaces.)
No, it's not a problem. It's just I get my nails done at one. You couldn't move the class to three?
(Under her breath.)
I don't know how you expect me to play volleyball with wet nails.
(Turns head.)

Section I: Reflections on 20-Century Jewish Life

Badminton? Please, don't insult me. Badminton is not "in" this year. It's like playing mahjongg with old tiles. You just don't do it.

(Annoyed.)

Audit? You want me to audit volleyball? I should sit and watch from the corner? Please, at my age I do enough sitting and watching. I don't have to go to school to be a bump on a log. I can do that on my own.

(Checks schedule.)

Wait...wait. What's this...

(Points at schedule.)

TM? *Vus a dus?* TM?

(She struggles with pronunciation.)

Transcendental meditation... A course in relaxation.

(Laughs.)

I can teach that. How to fall asleep in your chair when the news comes on. You call it TM? I call it Tom Brokaw... No...wait...I'll take it.

(Looks at paper in her hand.)

It fills a hole for me. What hole? Wednesday. Good. Now I only have six more holes to fill.

(Smiles.)

You're laughing. See? That's because I'm funny, right? I wasn't always funny, you know. It's because I took a comedy course last year. You know what was a blast? Mr. Goldenberg, who sat next to me. He had gas problems that kept the whole class awake, you should pardon the expression. A real walking billboard for Gelusil. Oh, we had a special name for him too. Let's just say it began with "Old" and leave it at that.

(Stares at wall.)

I see the Yiddish class is filled up.

(Laughs.)

Me? I know Yiddish like the back of my hand.

(Looks at hand absentmindedly.)

Another liver spot. Overnight, they come out. You turn your back on them and they sneak up on you and say, "Peek-a-boo! You're old!" Just like that.

(Suddenly tired.)

Oy! I've got to sit down.

(Approaches stool.)

They don't make these for a 75-year-old *tuchas*. Thirty years ago, I could have done this.

(Struggles to sit on it.)

Of course, thirty years ago I didn't wear orthopedic shoes, so I was closer to the ground. I've always said the day a woman starts wearing orthopedic shoes, she may as well announce to the world that it's all over. It's like getting up on a chair and yelling, "Hey, I can't keep up anymore!"

(Lifts up shoes to look at them.)

Did you ever see anything so *mishuga*?

(Grimaces, then rubs her legs.)

Old age?

(Defiantly.)

No. That's not the problem today. It was the aerobics. I overdid it again. Me and Richard Simmons, we're an item. He kvetches, I shvitz.

(Leans over, conspiratorially.)

Ever hear him on Howard Stern?

(Surprised.)

You don't know who Howard Stern is? It's the most disgusting show. I can't listen to it for more than an hour at a time. But at least I'm not afraid to listen, like some women

Section I: Reflections on 20-Century Jewish Life

I know. I'm hip. That's what my grandson tells me anyway. See this?

(Points to Grateful Dead T-shirt.)

He bought this for me, my grandson. He calls me Bobby. His father—my son, the attorney—said to him, "Stuart, how do you like your bubbie?" From then on, he calls me Bobby.

(Shrugs shoulders.)

That was eight years ago. I told them to check his hearing, but my daughter-in-law—may she rest in peace—says no, that it's not my concern. So, what do I care? It's not my business. I wash my hands of it. I don't bring it up again with my son's wife—may she rest in peace... Hmmm? No, she's still living, why do you ask?

(Pause.)

Anyway, my grandson, says to me. "Bobby, you're one happening mama. Real regular." Regular.

(Pause. Holds up hand.)

Let's not even talk about that... But, you know, at least I've got a life. Not like those other *yentas*. That's what Jackie Mason would call them... *yentas*. Sure, I saw his show. Three times. With three different ORT groups. Yeh. And I belong to two Hadassah chapters. Why? For the trips.

(Looks up.)

Wait, I'll take that one. What's it called? "Jews You Didn't Think Were Jewish." Maybe they'll tell me something I don't know. Like? After all these years—I just learned Jerry Lewis was Jewish. Imagine, Jerry Lewis a Jew.

(Frowns.)

Not exactly what I would call a victory for our side... You know, I could teach a class myself, I've taken so many of them... What could I teach? I could teach life. A class on how to mother—or how to smother, as my son used to say. He said I knew it better than anyone. Now, I can also teach how to play the bubba. Not that I get such a chance these days. Complaining? No, not me. My kids call like clockwork—if you got a clock that only works twice a year. No, it's fine. I have my life. Why do I need to mess up theirs?

(Straightens out hem of her shorts.)

I wouldn't have time for the kids even if they asked me... Besides, with all my courses, you think I could fit them in? I've taken crocheting, knitting, sewing... anything that ends in an "i-n-g" I take. My son says the only course left is *kvetching* and I already mastered that.

(Grimace.)

He's so funny. If they gave a degree just for me, he says it would be a masters of aggravation. An M.A. because it spells "Ma." He gets his sense of humor from me.

(Seriously.)

I'm funny when I have to be. Don't kid yourself, I know how to laugh. But, somehow, it sounds different bouncing off the walls in an efficiency apartment when the only noise you hear is yourself sneezing. Wait, I don't want you to think I don't have friends. Them I have plenty of. Mrs. Garfinkel, Mrs. Simon, Mrs. Robinson... No. Wait.

(Pause.)

She's dead. Mrs. Robinson's dead.

(Shakes head.)

Such a lovely funeral. Everyone turned out. All of her friends from the club. Her husband? He passed on years ago. That's why she joined the club. Some of these women will do anything to forget, to have company. You make friends. Friends who last your whole life—whatever's left of it. Like Mrs. Robinson and me. We were like this.

(Entwines her fingers gingerly.)

Her first name?

(Pause.)

I...never asked.

(Changing the subject.)

Say, is that mime you're offering again Friday afternoon? I took mime two years ago. Maybe three. Terrible. Terrible. They wouldn't let me talk. And what's a class without a little gossip?

(Laughs.)

If I wanted someone who didn't talk, I'd dig up my dead husband. Fine conversations we used to have. *Nu*, Saul? How was work? *"Nich te fellich,"* he'd say. *Nu*, Saul, what do you think of President Roosevelt's New Deal? "If it's good for the Jews, it's OK by me." *Nu*, Saul, what's the weather like tonight? "Dark." A scholar he wasn't.

(Softens.)

No, no. But... But, he had his moments. *Nu*, Saul, what do you think of my new blue dress?

(Stops, her eyes moist with memory.)

"It's beautiful, Sara. Just like you."

(Grows somewhat softer, smiling a bit.)

He had a way, my Saul... So maybe he wasn't an Einstein. I never wanted a man with such messy hair anyway. Saul, let's go to the movies, I'd say. "OK, Sara, if that will make you happy." He did. He made me happy. He used to listen to me play the piano for hours and then he'd say, "Sara, please don't stop. I could listen to you forever." He would always tell me that I was the one in the family with the smarts, with the talent... He was the one with the heart... Did I tell you about our forty-fifth anniversary?

(Smiles; she seems to be growing younger.)

You know what he did? He took me dancing. Dancing. For the first time in our lives. Oh, he would step on my feet occasionally—*oy*, do you know what it's like to have someone give a *shtup* to a hammer toe? I said, Saul, Saul, you're no Fred Astaire. And do you know what he said to me? He said, "Sara, that's OK, that's OK, because he only had Ginger Rogers and I have you. For that I'm luckier than Fred Astaire."

(Smiles.)

He said that. My Saulie. I guess that's why I loved him. He swept me off my feet.

(Listens intently.)

A prince? He was a king. But...

(Whisking away imaginary lint from her shorts.)

...even kings don't live up to their word. And I never forgave him for that.

(Listens.)

Hmm? No. I'd rather not get into it.

(Taken aback.)

Cheat? Did Saul cheat? No. Of course not. He was a Jewish husband. No, my Saulie was a good man... How did he lie?

(Long pause.)

What does it matter now?

(Long pause.)

He always told me that no matter what, "No matter what, Sara," he said, "I will always be there for you." My protector, that's what he called himself. My other lady friends, whose husbands fell asleep on the sofa watching reruns of

Love Connection, they'd scream in their ears, trying to wake them up, "Be like Saul! Be like Saul!"

(Softly.)

Be like Saul.

(Pause.)

Our children, they grew up, they moved out. I never had time to be lonely because Saul was there for me. Always. "And I always will be," he told me. And then, just like that, he...wasn't. It wasn't the way we planned it. Death never is... It...wasn't the way we planned it at all.

(Directly.)

Do you know what loneliness is?

(Doubtful.)

Do you?

(Shakes head.)

I'll tell you what it is. It's an old lady buying soup for one and freezing half of it. It's making new lady friends so you have someplace to go on a Saturday. The couples you used to go out with Saturday night you don't see anymore. The ones who still have husbands don't want to be reminded what's in store for them. And those that don't, well...they just stop calling. You stop calling. Everyone...stops. And suddenly, there's...nothing.

(Smiles.)

No, Saulie, as much as he loved me, he went back on his word. He left me. Alone. And I'll never forgive him for that.

(Sarcastically.)

So, tell me, on that big schedule of yours, with all these fancy courses, do you have anyone here who can teach me to deal with that?

(Shakes her head, closing her eyes. Long pause. Slowly, sadly, she breaks away from her memories. Back to registrar, brushing back tears.)

So, what's that, Thursday at three? Bungee jumping?

(Pause.)

You jump from a WHAT?

(Sighs.)

All right. Sign me up. Maybe I'll start out easy...like getting up from a chair. Look, it couldn't be worse than physical therapy. I could use a good scream. What have I got to lose?

(Looks at her own schedule.)

Say, what do you have Monday at one? I've got some time to kill. Anything at two? *Nu*, how about three?

(Nods head as she listens to registrar. Fade to black.)

END

WHERE'S YOUR STUFF?
by Daniel Brenner

CHARACTERS:

BEN
JENNIFER
CANTOR

SETTING: *We are in the humble home of BEN and JENNIFER.*

AT RISE: *It is the middle of the night.*

BEN *(screaming, sitting up in bed)*. Aaaaaaaaahhh!
JENNIFER. Ahhhhh! *(Both return to sleep.)*
BEN. Arrrrhhhhhh!
JENNIFER. What is it, Ben?
BEN. It's the bar mitzvah dream.
JENNIFER. It's just a bad dream, honey.
BEN. I can't sleep.
JENNIFER. Come on Benny-baby, we have to be at La Guardia at seven-thirty tomorrow. Get some sleep.
BEN. It's a giant bobbing head of my old cantor... Cantor Birnsomething... Birnstein... Birnberg... Birnowitz... Birnman... Birn...
JENNIFER. Birnbaum. Cantor Birnbaum. he died two years ago in that bizarre stamp-collecting accident.
BEN. What?

JENNIFER. Don't worry about it, baby. Just come back under the covers and curl up beside me.
BEN. I just wanna get a glass of seltzer. *(He kisses her.)* Zorro will return!
JENNIFER. Don't take long!

(BEN walks to the kitchen, turns on the light to reveal CANTOR BIRNBAUM, gently kissing a large kosher salami he has found.)

BEN. Cantor Birnbaum?
CANTOR. Shaa! Shhh. Benjamin Adam Levy! You look just like you did on your bar mitzvah day!
BEN. Uhhh... you're dead.
CANTOR. Do I look that bad?
BEN. What are you doing in my kitchen?
CANTOR. You know what I'm here for. I've been visiting you in your dreams for weeks, telling you: Benjie! You skipped an entire paragraph of your *haftorah* portion! Such a thing doesn't go unnoticed. Now... what do you got to eat around here.
BEN. This isn't happening. I don't know how you got here, but you're dead... and you're in my house.
CANTOR. You are absolutely right.
BEN. Cantor, I'm a man now. What do you want from me?
CANTOR. A pickle, some herring, whaddya got?
JENNIFER *(calling from bedroom)*. Honey, I'm waiting for you!
BEN *(whispers)*. Just leave me alone.
CANTOR. Fine. I just want to *nosh*. And we have to talk.

Section I: Reflections on 20-Century Jewish Life 21

BEN. My wife is calling me. You wanna pickle? Have a pickle! I'm forgetting that this happened. Goodbye. *(BEN returns to bed.)*

JENNIFER. What took you so long?

BEN. Uhh. Nothing. Come here, baby... *(He starts to caress her as the CANTOR begins to chant the* haftorah *in the next room. BEN sits up.)*

JENNIFER. What?

BEN. Do you hear that?

JENNIFER. What?

BEN. You don't hear anything?

JENNIFER. No, I hear you freaking-out at nearly two in the morning. That's what I hear. Forget it, Ben. I'm going back to sleep.

BEN. I'm sorry. Good night, baby. *(BEN gets up slowly, sneaks into the kitchen.)* Cantor Birnbaum, you can't do this! You can't be here!

CANTOR. OK, I'll chant quietly.

BEN *(sitting beside the CANTOR)*. Why are you doing this to me?

CANTOR. Listen, Ben. I'm dead. Stiff as a week-old *challah*. I can't even pass gas anymore. And, you're not going to believe this, but heaven is just like the Goyim say it is! All day, angels playing harps and flutes, singing Hallelujah! Hallelujah! Hallelujah! Aaacchhh! It's no place for a Jew! No card playing, no *New York Times*, no *borscht*! And all the great Jewish entertainers are down there, gorging themselves on pork products and copulating with six-breasted she-beasts! It may be hot, but they are living all my fantasies! Me, I've got nothing to do until the Mosiach comes, so I'm working out some unfinished business. That's why I'm here.

BEN. Look, Cantor, I know that you mean well, but how do I say this: I'm not really Jewish anymore.

CANTOR What?

BEN. I'm Unitarian. Unitarian Universalist.

CANTOR. So, that explains the question mark the Klan was burning on your lawn.

BEN *(laughs).* Cantor, my *bar mitzvah* meant nothing to me. I was thirteen years old. I was in it for the money. I mean, how did you expect me to learn to chant some ancient Hebrew?

CANTOR. Maybe if you didn't play with yourself so much, you would have learned.

BEN. How did you know? Oh, forget it. Cantor—I don't believe in the Jewish religion.

CANTOR. It's not a matter of belief, Benjie. You are a Jew. The *haftorah* is part of your history, the history of your people, your ancestors. That's a fact. You come from a proud—

BEN. Wait. What are you trying to tell me?

CANTOR. Ben, you used to come to *shul* with your father every week. How could you not remember something good?

BEN. You know what I remember, I remember the last time I thought about going to synagogue. Freshman year of college. A bus from Hillel was supposed to stop by the dorm to go for Rosh Hashanah. I waited for two hours in a three-piece suit for that bus to show up, and all the time I'm thinking, who am I doing this for, huh? I don't want to go to these services. I don't believe in this God. The only reason I was going was that I thought that I might meet some nice Jewish girl or something. Then I met Jennifer. She's not Jewish. She asked me to play guitar for a solstice service at the Unitarian Church, and you know what? I liked it. We did stuff from all sorts of cultures and religions. It was...I don't know...it was different. It made me feel free; feel like I fit in.

CANTOR. But where's your stuff?

BEN. What do you mean?

CANTOR. Do you know what a *neshama* is?

BEN. A *neshama*?

CANTOR. Yes. A *neshama*. Your soul, Ben. You have a Jewish *neshama*. You know what that means? You were a slave in Egypt! You journeyed to the Promised Land! You brought the first fruits of your harvest to Jerusalem! You took part in creating a society built on justice! You sang songs of freedom, of loss, of celebration, and even when you were taken from your land, you carried these songs with you. And they are still with you. These are your songs, Ben. Your *neshama*.

BEN. So a *neshama* is a Jewish soul?

CANTOR. It is *your* soul, Ben.

BEN. Why are you telling me this now?

CANTOR. I wasn't going to tell you this, but I know something about you and Jennifer.

BEN. What?

CANTOR. It's good news. You're going to have a child soon.

BEN. How do you know?

CANTOR. You have coffee with God and she tells you things. Trust me, Ben. You have a song to learn, to teach your child to sing.

BEN. The *haftorah*?

CANTOR. We'll start where you left off. OK?

BEN. OK.

CANTOR. Repeat after me. *Baruch Atah.*
BEN. *Baruch Atah.*
CANTOR. *Adoshem Elohaynoo*
BEN. *Adoshem Elohaynoo*
CANTOR. *Melech Ha-o-laam*
BEN. *Melech Ha-o-laam*

(JENNIFER walks in.)

JENNIFER. Jesus Christ, Ben! What's going on here?
BEN. Jen, I'm practicing my *haftorah*. We'll try to be quieter.
JENNIFER. *We'll* be quieter?
BEN. Yes, Jennifer, this is Cantor Birnbaum.
JENNIFER. Where? Are you sleepwalking? There is nobody here, Ben!
CANTOR. Should I come back later?
BEN. No, stay.
JENNIFER. Who are you talking to?
BEN. You can't see the cantor? He's right here!
JENNIFER. Wake up, Ben! Wake up!
BEN. I'm awake.
JENNIFER. You're losing it again. I'm calling Dr. Berman right now. This is scary, Ben! This is really scary!
CANTOR. Look, she's upset. I'll leave.
BEN. I'm starting to enjoy this.
CANTOR. OK, *Ah-sher. Been-vee-neem.*
BEN. OK, *Ah-sher. Been-vee-neem. (They continue chanting.)*
JENNIFER. Hello, Dr. Berman, I'm sorry to wake you, but this is Jennifer Barret-Levy, and Ben is flipping out. He's sleepwalking or talking or I don't know—he's just out of his mind... You've got to come down and talk some sense into him... I can't talk to him... Yes... uh-

huh... yes... oh... thank you, Doctor, thank you so much... OK... bye.

CANTOR. You have a gorgeous voice, Benjie.

BEN. Thanks. I love singing. It's the only part of Hebrew school I could stand.

CANTOR. Hey, do you remember Miss Shapiro?

BEN. How could I forget, the woman punished me for weeks.

CANTOR. What did she make you do?

BEN. She force-fed me kosher for Passover ketchup. It was horrible.

CANTOR. Well, let me tell you, Ben, I took her to that sisterhood dinner dance, the uh... the Matza Ball, and let's put it this way—when I saw her shake her booty... I elevated myself before the Lord.

BEN. So, anything happen between you two?

CANTOR. Let's put it this way. We did things in a minivan that threw my back out for a week.

BEN. Cantor, I'm glad you came to see me.

CANTOR. Me too. Ben, inside you is a still, small voice. It calls you to return to the tribal ways. It misses you, Benjie.

BEN. I hear it.

CANTOR. Good. Now it's late. I've got some other people to see. Good night, Benjie.

BEN. Wait. I want to give you something, a gift... here, take these. *(He hands him the pickles.)*

CANTOR. Thanks. You are very kind. *(Bell rings. JENNIFER runs to answer it.)*

JENNIFER. Dr. Berman, thank God!

CANTOR. Berman? Marvin Schlomo Berman— You look just like you did on your bar mitzvah day! *(Lights fade.)*

END

THE FOOT PEDDLER
by Vivian Green

CHARACTERS:

TOM: A young man.

SETTING: *The bedroom of a small rowhouse in South Philadelphia. It is the late 19th century. We hear the one-sided conversation TOM is having with his wife, Fanny, who is offstage, in bed.*

TOM

—Give me a few minutes, Fanny. I'll come to bed as soon as I soak my feet. Some week I had, Fanny...four days of freezing rain...struggling up and down muddy roads with that cursed trunk strapped to my back...as heavy as if it were filled with stones instead of needles and pins. I tell you, Fanny, my bones can't take this life. I'm twenty-seven years old but I feel like ninety.

(Is it my fault?)

—Of course not. Why should I blame you? If not for your family, I would be nothing. Could I ever forget how your Uncle Jacob and Tante Sima-Leah took me in when I was a greenhorn fresh off the boat? Introduced me to their red-haired niece...started me in business? I owe everything to you.

Section I: Reflections on 20-Century Jewish Life

It's just...I get so tired, Fanny. If only I had a horse and wagon. With a horse and wagon... God willing, in a few years... by the turn of the century.

(So tell me what happened!)

—I will tell you! I'll tell you the whole story...in my own way. Why are you always so impatient?

(Why do you drag things out?)

—Maybe I do tend to drag things out a little, but tonight I have a good reason. If I begin at the beginning and tell you everything, maybe you'll understand. I went as far as Springfield. My biggest sale was to a farmer's wife near Newton. She took half a dozen shirt collars...three cotton bonnets...a bottle of glue...and a pair of spectacles. A farmer near Quakertown cleaned out the roach and fly traps...remind me to stock up before I go out again...oh...a grocer near Bensalem took three dozen candles and half a dozen mustard plasters. That was a good idea you had about the playing cards, Fanny. They went like hotcakes.

(Where did you sleep?)

—Where I always sleep...in barns with the mice and the horse manure.

(While I'm living on easy street?)

—No...no, Fanny, who said you're living on easy street? I know how hard you work. Please, God, by the time the baby gets here, we'll have enough put by so you can give up dressmaking. If I'm complaining, Fanny, it's because I want you to know how cold and wet I was all week...and then you'll understand why I...

(Where was your waterproof?)

—Even with my waterproof. Nothing could keep out such a deluge. Didn't it rain in Philadelphia?

(Cats and dogs.)

—Then you know what I'm talking about. What kept me going like a horse headed for its stall, was the dream of our soft bed with the thick feather quilt...and your sweet little body next to mine as warm as an oven. And that's why I landed in trouble.

(What trouble?!!)

—I'm trying to tell you! Yesterday a farmer offered me a lift to Millboro, so I decided to take a chance on catching the ten o'clock train...instead of spending another night on the road. Even with Uncle and Tante up the block from us, I still worry about you. Fanny, in your condition, you shouldn't be alone.

(The train!)

—What...? What did you say?

(The train!)

—Oh...the train! I missed it by one hour. Fanny, I could have kicked myself into the next county. A whole year in service and I have yet to get a ride on that train. So there I was...stuck in a strange town late at night...with no place

Section I: Reflections on 20-Century Jewish Life

to lay my head...and rain pouring down as if God meant to drown the world a second time.

(Didn't they have an inn?)

—Yes, they did...the King George...a fine inn with Turkish carpets on the floor and a fire in the fireplace. I could smell pea soup. My mouth was watering. I had visions of a four-poster bed. The the innkeeper told me they were full up. Maybe yes...maybe no. Maybe he just didn't like the way I tracked mud on his carpet. *(Coins drop out of his pockets as he is taking off his pants. He crawls around on the floor, picking up coins.)*

(What was that?)

—Nothing...nothing...some coins fell out of my pocket.

(So? Where did you sleep?)

—Don't rush me, my little firebrand. I'll tell you where I slept in a minute. I trudged up and down the slippery brick sidewalks looking for a boarding house...Mulberry Street...Grundy...River Road...not a sign anywhere... not a sound...not a light...I could have been in the land of the dead. My teeth were chattering and my feet were frozen. The trunk weighed me down to the ground.

(It was your own fault!)

—You're so right, Fanny, it *was* my own fault. You're always telling me I leave too much to chance and you're absolutely right. I came to a tavern: The Turk's Head. Before I could open the door, four men tumbled out...wild animals, yelling at the top of their lungs. I slipped into the shadows. Too late! A giant with shoulders like an ox caught hold of me. "Why are you hanging around here, Jew-boy?" Then he tugged at the trunk straps. "Come on, men, let's see what he has in the trunk." "Take off your hand," I told him. He laughed in my face. Yeech! He stank from beer! "Take off my hand? I need my hand to teach you a good lesson, Jew-boy!" Then he gave me a punch in the face with a fist like a blacksmith's hammer. Everything went dark before my eyes. When I came to, I was lying in the gutter with the open trunk beside me. My head was throbbing and I had a big lump on my forehead. Fanny, I never felt so wretched. For this I left my folks in Kolbeshev and came to America?! My soul cried out to heaven: "Master of the Universe, what have I done to deserve such misery?"

(Tevya, come to bed.)

—Soon...soon...as soon as I soak my feet. *(He drapes the blanket around his shoulders and puts his feet into the basin.)* Aahh...aahh...

(Is the water hot enough?)

—Yes...it's hot enough.

(So? Nu? Finish!)

—Give me a chance, Fanny...I'm getting there...just don't keep interrupting. Where was I...?

(In the gutter.)

—Oh...the gutter. I crawled around on my hands and knees trying to find everything...they stole all the knives...a

Section I: Reflections on 20-Century Jewish Life

plague on them! Then I heard a horse's hooves clopping on the cobblestones. I leaped in front of the horse and the driver pulled in the reins just in time. "Hey! Are you crazy?" "Lodgings," I cried. "Do you know of any lodgings?" A woman stuck her head out of the buggy. "What happened to you, mister?" "Hoodlums," I told her. "I'm a foot peddler and I have no place to stay." She said, "You can come home with me," and I thought my prayers had been answered.

(Woman? What woman?)

—I don't know, Fanny, just a woman. It was dark in the buggy so I didn't get a good look at her. There was a thin rug on the floor and I stuck my icy feet under it. We drove past the Millboro Lumber and Roofing Company at the edge of town and then we turned down a side street to a rowhouse with a gate hanging by one hinge. I had a better look at her when she put her key in the door...a nice-looking *shiksa*...not young but...never mind that part. When she opened the door and I saw the room with its big bed, I could have kissed her.

(Kissed her?!)

—Fanny, why don't you listen? You never listen! I said I *could* have kissed her. The room wasn't as cozy as our bedroom. Rain tapped into a pail in the corner...but it was warm and clean.

(What did she charge you?)

—Fifty cents for the night...and worth every penny. I was so grateful I opened the trunk and told her to help herself.

(Mr. Generous!)

—Fanny, the woman saved my life! It was the least I could do. Don't worry...she took only a few pairs of cotton and woolen hose. Better her than a hoodlum. She offered me a cup of tea and a slice of sourdough bread. Mmm...delicious! Nothing ever tasted as good...except for your cooking, it goes without saying, Fanny. She told me to call her Cora. When I told her my name, she wouldn't believe me...so I had to explain how that comedian on Castle Garden changed my name from Tevya Goldovsky to Thomas Jefferson Gold...and that gave her a good laugh.

(So you had a high old time while I was working myself to the bone.)

—Just a few friendly words, Fanny. What...you think I was enjoying myself? Fanny, I was more dead than alive.

(Tevya! What happened?!)

—I'm getting there...I'm getting there...I'm almost to the end. I was waiting for her to leave so I could fall into bed. Instead...she began to...unbutton her blouse...

(I knew it!)

—You knew?! Then you're smarter than I am because...

(You knew!)

—No, Fanny, I swear to God I didn't even suspect it.

(Don't swear!)

—All right, I won't swear...you'll just have to believe me. I said to her: "Cora, I made a mistake. I'm a married man.

My wife is expecting. Possibly you have another room...?"
"The rest of the house is occupied," she said. "Suit yourself, Tom. You already paid me, so you can get into bed or sit up in that chair. Lord knows, I can use a good rest." Then she climbed into bed and pulled the blanket over her head.

(What did you do?)

—I sat in the chair.

(All night?)

—No...not the whole night. *(He covers his ears.)* —Wait! Wait a minute! Let me finish before you start to scream. Fanny, I was on the verge of collapse. My head was in a whirl and my legs were like pillars of stone. When the woman began to snore, I eased a pillow into the middle of the bed and I crept in...and in a minute, I was asleep. Before the sun came up, I was out of the house. I fixed the broken hinge on the gate and then I went on my way. And that's the whole story, Fanny, so now you know. If you want to run home to your uncle's house, who could blame you? But, Fanny...if you think I would ever lie to you...if you think I would ever dishonor you... *(He hurriedly dries his feet.)* —Fanny, please don't cry! —What? —Laughing? Fanny, dear! *(Rushes off to Fanny.)*

END

SMOKE

by Louis Greenstein

CHARACTERS:

MAN

AT RISE: *A MAN sits center stage. He holds an unlit cigar.*

MAN

Do we remember our parents—or their parents—as they actually were? Or have we created their memories to suit our needs, so that we can make sense of stuff?

When I remember, am I re-creating the people and events of my life as they actually were? Am I creating something entirely new? Or, is it a little of both?

(He regards the cigar.)

In a few minutes I'm going to light up. You may not care for the smell of a cigar. I can sympathize, but in this case, I think the end—ah, no pun intended—justifies the means. Psychologists say that smell is our most powerful sense in relation to memory. The smell of something can evoke memories and emotions much more potently than the sight or sound or touch of it. Psychologists say things about cigars, too. Freud, a lifelong-cigar smoker, once said, sometimes a cigar is just a cigar.

Section I: Reflections on 20-Century Jewish Life 35

An actor once described to me how to create actual emotions while onstage. This is what he told me: Onstage, he said, your lover walks out on you. The script calls for you to burst into tears. Now, in real life when your lover walks out on you, you don't burst into tears; you open the fridge and you make yourself a salami sandwich. You sit down and begin eating. Halfway through the sandwich you realize your lover is gone, and *then* you burst into tears. So onstage, when your lover walks out, and the script tells you to cry, you draw in a breath and you re-create the smell of salami. And you cry.

One day a few months ago I was walking past a tobacco shop. I pass this shop every day on my way to work. I don't smoke; that is, on that particular day a few months ago, I didn't smoke. There was no reason for me to enter the store. But that day, that's exactly what I did. Now, there I was, standing in this tobacco shop, and a woman behind the counter said, Can I help you, and I paused for a moment because I really didn't know what I was doing there. I told her that I wanted a cigar. Now, I am an impulsive guy, but this was weird even for me. The woman sent me back to a humidor room stocked with thousands of cigars from all over the world. There was an old guy in there, and I told him I had never smoked a cigar, and I asked him to sell me one. Here's one to start with, he told me, and I paid him two bucks for a Julia Marlowe, hand rolled in the Dominican Republic. He asked if I wanted him to clip the end. Sure, I said, not knowing exactly what he was talking about.

   (*He takes a cigar clipper from his pocket, inspects the cigar, then carefully clips the end off its tip. He muses.*)

Boy's first cigar.

What in the world was I gonna tell my wife? That it followed me home? I told her I had a confession to make. What have you done, she asked? I took the cigar from my pocket and I showed it to her. She looked at it. She looked at me. She looked back at it. If you smoke that in the house, she said, I will kill you; then I will divorce you.

That night, after dinner, I took my pet cigar out to the front porch. It was a breezy summer evening. I didn't know what to expect. I couldn't imagine the allure of puffing on a cigar. What could the appeal be? I lit it up and took a puff. I held the smoke in my mouth for a moment, then gently puffed it back out into the summer air. The smell of the burning leaves overcame me and I was transported. In that moment, as the smoke flitted off into the darkness, my senses were overwhelmed. Suddenly I remembered something. My father smoked cigars! Now, I have a pretty good memory; in fact, I have a damn good memory. People I run into from high school, maybe I haven't seen them in twenty years but I remember details of their lives, conversations I had with them. I remember my childhood and my mother and father so clearly. They're dead now; she in 1970. He, seven years later. I have an excellent memory, but I didn't remember that my dad smoked a cigar until I lit one up myself, until I tasted the smoke, and in a flash, there he was, standing on the boardwalk in Atlantic City, leaning against the railing, relaxed, content, and puffing on a cigar. He had a way of puckering his lips, and letting the smoke drift out ever so gently. He savored that smoke, and I had had no recollection until that moment. That night, on my porch, it all came back.

What else don't I remember about my father? What don't you remember about yours? Was he loving, but you won't remember his love until you yourself love? Was he violent, but you won't remember until you raise a hand to your kid?

I took a second puff and tasted the smoke. Rich. Sweet. My sense of taste became stimulated. It's like a fine wine, I realized, like brandy. To be savored. I've seen wine-tasting exhibitions, and I know that the judges do not swallow; they taste the wine then spit it out. With a cigar, too, the smoke is not consumed, not inhaled, but merely tasted, exposed to the sensory organs then released. Savored then released, offered up, as it were... like a prayer.

My kids came out to the porch to see what Daddy was doing. They were mesmerized by the sight of me smoking. I let out little puffs then managed a smoke ring. My kids chased the rings, and tried to put their fingers through them. OOOO's they said, OOOO's, Daddy's making smoke O's. Try an S, said Sam. And I remembered chasing my father's smoke rings, and watching them drift off into nothingness. I loved chasing his smoke rings, poking my finger through them. How could I not have remembered doing that?

How will my children remember me? Will they forget chasing my smoke rings? What else don't I remember?
With each puff I drew in the memory of my father—his scent, his pleasure, his breath. With each puff I exhaled his life, the life of a salesman lived on interstates between sales calls, listening to Frank Sinatra and Tommy Dorsey tapes, and smoking cigars. After my mother died, on days when I had off from school, I used to have to ride with him. I

wanted to be back in the neighborhood with my friends, but he didn't want me home alone. I wouldn't let him smoke when I was in the car. He would offer to blow it out the window, and I would offer to stay home. I'd say, Dad I'm 12 years old, I'm OK on my own. You wanna smoke that, just lemme stay home like my friends. He'd say, Your friends have mothers at home to take care of them. And he'd say he was sorry. Anyway, it was all right; I loved Sinatra. But God how I hated those cigars!

Today I am a cigar smoker. One cigar a week. Only on Friday nights after dinner. I am not a religious Jew. Yet, somehow, this is my way of honoring the Sabbath and keeping it separate from the other days. It sounds crazy, I know. Why is this night different from all other nights? Or maybe it isn't so crazy. On this night I invoke my father's spirit; I am the connection between my father and my children.

Maybe spirituality is as mundane as a leaf wrapped up in more leaves, and clipped and placed in the mouth and ignited. Maybe the simple ritual of tobacco is as spiritually significant as a prayer. Suppose you pray, but you're not really paying attention while you do it. There you are, talking to God, and if God actually talked back, you wouldn't notice because you weren't paying attention. This may have happened to some of us. Now, what if you are sitting on your porch, enjoying your cigar, very focused and calm. And while you smoke you contemplate the stars in the sky and the dampness in the air, and the mosquitoes buzzing and the wind, invisible, carrying your smoke swirling off to God-knows-where. You are content and silent. Your breathing is steady, and you are so tuned in to the stillness of the evening, you think that when you release your next wisp of smoke you will dissolve with it into the eternity of the night. You think the wind is the breath of God, and as you breathe with it you draw inspiration. This moment is perfect. It is the Sabbath, the day of rest. The candles are burning; the wine was sweet and the brisket tender; all week long you have toiled and now the sun is down and the kids are in bed and your wife is singing softly somewhere in the house. Puffing a cigar on the front porch, exploring your memory, creating your dreams, knowing that the soul of your father is right there beside you, you are one with all the world.

(He lights the cigar, and draws a puff. As he exhales, the lights fade to black.)

END

Section II:
A Minyan of Women

SINGLE JEWISH FEMALE
by Julianne Bernstein

CHARACTERS:

TEDDY: In her 50s.
LEON: In his mid-30s.
MISSIE: In her 30s.

SETTING: *Friday afternoon at the office of the* Weekly Kosher Catch—*a newspaper.*

AT RISE: *TEDDY is working at the desk.*

TEDDY *(on phone).* I know! You'll get your money! You'll all get your money. Hold on. I got another call. *(She hangs up the phone and puts a piece of paper in the typewriter and starts to type.)* Dear Terribly Troubled. *(The phone rings again.)* The *Weekly Kosher Catch*, can I help you? What? No way. I'm not bumping the lead story for this week. *(Pause.)* I don't care if he is attending services at your place. Ah, please. I got letters to write—lives to save. *(Hangs up.)* Fancy Schmancy Press Secretary to the President. Well! *(Looking at a framed picture on her desk.)* Oh, Abe. I want to be with you. I don't want this life no more. I want to be with you.

(LEON enters. He wears an open vest, and is beside himself after a hard day's work at the paper.)

43

LEON. Teddy, where's my tie? *(Sees her staring at the picture.)* What's with you?

TEDDY. Abe wants to move to Bermuda.

LEON. And he wants you to go with him?

TEDDY. No. He's taking his other wife of twenty-two years. Of course he wants me to go with him.

LEON. *Gay ga zunta hey**. Where the heck is my tie?

TEDDY. Did you look in the refrig?

LEON. The refrig?

TEDDY. Your tie.

LEON. My tie's in the refrig?

TEDDY. It's broken. We gotta use it for something.

LEON. Let's fix it before we start using it as a closet.

TEDDY. Fix it with what, Leon? We're broke. We haven't paid our salaries since Moses and the bush.

LEON. I know, I know. But ads are pickin' up.

(MISSIE enters the office, wearing a dark coat and sunglasses; she's so mousy that LEON and TEDDY don't notice her, not even her feeble attempts to get their attention.)

TEDDY. Your sister called. She wants you should bring flowers.

LEON. Then spot me a ten out of the petty cash— I'll get some roses.

TEDDY *(handing him change out of a cigar box)*. Here. Pick out a packet of seeds.

LEON. This is barely bus fare.

* Translation: go in good health

Section II: A Minyan of Women

TEDDY. Oh, yeah. She also said to bring the playset for the boys.

LEON. They're not gettin' it until Hanukkah. I told 'em. Besides, it's all in parts—and I spilled seltzer all over the directions.

TEDDY. You need to get out more, Leon. You need to get married.

LEON. Agh! WHERE'S MY TIE?!!! *(He exits.)*

TEDDY *(looking at the picture).* Oh, Abe. I know I promised his mother, but...but...such a mess!

MISSIE *(breaking out).* Excuse me!

TEDDY. Oh, God. Hello, hello, hello. What can I do for you? You want to buy a subscription?

MISSIE. No.

TEDDY. You wanna buy ad space?

MISSIE *(quietly).* Not exactly.

TEDDY. You got some pressing news for our readers—like you're Henny Penny and the world is gonna explode?

MISSIE *(inaudible).* I want to place a personal.

TEDDY. What?

MISSIE. A personal ad.

TEDDY. I can't hear you, darling, speak up.

MISSIE. A personal.

TEDDY. A personal? *(MISSIE nods. TEDDY shouts to back.)* LEON, COME OUT! I GOT A LONER UP FRONT! *(Pause.)* Leon's in charge of the personals. Me? I answer calls, letters, and any question you got about the newspaper, the community, what's this week's special down at Glatt's. Take off your coat.

MISSIE. I don't feel well.

TEDDY. Then take off your coat.

(LEON enters, wiping his hands.)

LEON. No tie. All I found was my Budget Gourmet Lunch and a melted Jello Pop. Where's a napkin? *(To MISSIE.)* And what's with the coat?

MISSIE. I'm sick.

LEON. Then take off your coat. *(MISSIE stands frozen but starts to hyperventilate.)* Oh my God. What's wrong?

TEDDY. She's here to place a personal.

LEON. But what's she doing now? I mean—like right now.

TEDDY. I don't know.

LEON. She's suffocating in her own coat. We gotta do something.

MISSIE. I'm gonna be sick. I gotta go! *(She covers her mouth with her hand.)*

TEDDY. The nearest bathroom's at the twenty-four hour convenient place—but you gotta pick up the key from this zitty-eared fellow named Marcus.

MISSIE. I'm sick. I'm very, very sick!

LEON *(points to the back)*. Follow the trail of Jewish New Year's cards! *(MISSIE exits.)* I'm going after her.

TEDDY. She probably wants her privacy.

LEON. Who's gonna hold her hair?

TEDDY. What?

LEON. If she's throwin' up—someone's gotta hold her hair.

TEDDY. You'd hold her hair?

LEON *(looking off towards the bathroom)*. Somebody's got to.

TEDDY. But you? Have you held hair before?

LEON *(ignoring TEDDY)*. I'm gonna go see. *(He exits.)*

TEDDY. Abe? It wouldn't hurt to make an appointment with the broker in Bermuda. It wouldn't hurt one bit.

(LEON reenters.)

TEDDY. Well?
LEON. She locked herself in.
TEDDY. *Oy!*

(MISSIE enters.)

LEON. How ya feeling?
MISSIE. I've never done this before.
LEON. So? For fifteen dollars you can dare to be bold.
TEDDY. I think she meant gettin' sick.
MISSIE. No. He's right. I never placed an ad. I never even been on a date before.
TEDDY. Where've you been till now?
MISSIE *(quickly)*. Pre, nursery, elementary, junior high and high school, M.A., M.B.A., Ph.D., and now I'm a C.P.A. with an AMX card —corporate gold.
LEON. We prefer cash.
TEDDY. Leon.
LEON. What? I'm supposed to rollerblade over to my sister's for Shabbas? I still gotta pay for flowers. Fifteen dollars could take care of my whole evening and leave a little change in my pocket. Gimme the ad, lady.
TEDDY. She's got a name, I'm sure.
MISSIE. It's Missie.
LEON. OK, lady. Missie, I mean. Missie-lady, lady-Missie. Gimme what you wrote.
TEDDY. Go ahead, Missie. You're in good hands. Real good hands. *(MISSIE finally hands them the ad.)*
LEON. But all you got here is SJF.
TEDDY. That's Single Jewish Female.

LEON. I know, I know.

MISSIE. That's all I could think to say.

LEON. SJF? That's it? But nobody'll call you with an ad like this.

MISSIE. I changed my mind. This is no way to meet someone. It's just too late.

LEON. Too late?

MISSIE. Yesterday, I turned 33.

LEON. So? *Nu?* You'll treat yourself to a fifteen-dollar personal for your birthday. Happy birthday.

MISSIE *(attacking him)*. NOT TODAY! IT WAS YESTERDAY, YOU IDIOT! YOU MORON! DO YOU ALWAYS WISH PEOPLE A HAPPY BIRTHDAY THE DAY *AFTER* THEIR BIRTHDAY? WHAT ARE YOU? MENTAL?!!!

LEON. Hey, I don't need this.

TEDDY. You do, Leon. You do. Believe me, you do.

LEON. This abuse? Ha! Forget it.

TEDDY. What about the cash?

LEON *(moving toward the door)*. I'll walk to my sister's.

TEDDY. But the flowers.

LEON. I'll bring her some mulch. I'm outta here.

TEDDY. Leon, stay.

MISSIE. Yeah, Leon—stay. *(He looks at her.)*

TEDDY. Missie probably works with a lot of very nice single people.

MISSIE. One hundred and seven.

LEON. How do you know?

MISSIE. Social functions. Holiday parties. I notice rings and spouses. I take a count.

LEON. You count the rings?

TEDDY. And there're many single folk who could use our services. Right, Missie? *(MISSIE cries.)* Oh, dear.

Section II: A Minyan of Women

LEON. Are you gonna be sick again?

MISSIE. I don't know.

TEDDY *(pause)*. You want Leon should hold your hair?

MISSIE. What?

TEDDY. Forget it. Leon will compose another ad for you. He's an expert at composing ads for people. A regular Irvin Berlin, he is.

LEON. Pardon me?

TEDDY. He's received many awards and *accommodations* for his work. He'll write you an ad so attractive you'll get a hundred dates...a thousand men...calling you...for the chance to ask you for a date. There'll be so many, they'll have to take a number.

MISSIE. Oh! I'm gonna be sick again!

LEON. No—no. Don't be sick. Sit down. Breathe. I'll write an ad for you. It'll be nice. And you'll get a call. One—maybe two calls. A nice, manageable number of calls.

MISSIE *(pause)*. OK, but keep it simple.

LEON. No problem. Now. What is it you like to do?

MISSIE. What do you mean?

TEDDY. You like to cook? You like to listen to music? You like to go to the movies?

MISSIE. I love to go to the movies.

TEDDY. Good, good. The movies. Write that down, Leon.

LEON *(writes)*. Likes the movies.

TEDDY. Loves to go to the movies.

MISSIE. Alone.

LEON. You're missing the point, Missie.

TEDDY. What do you like most about yourself?

MISSIE. Oh, God, please don't make me.

LEON. OK, forget about you. What're you looking for in a man?

MISSIE. I don't know.

LEON. You don't know?!!

MISSIE. Don't yell at me.

TEDDY. Don't yell.

MISSIE. What do you look for—in a woman, I mean?

TEDDY. He doesn't look.

LEON. What do you mean? I placed an ad, once.

MISSIE. You did?

LEON. Well, yeah. It's my paper. I got it free. *(The phone rings.)*

TEDDY *(turning away)*. You two keep talking.

MISSIE. So? What happened?

LEON. With what?

MISSIE. The ad.

LEON. I got a few calls.

MISSIE. How many?

LEON. A couple. A few.

MISSIE. How many?

TEDDY *(still on the phone)*. Nine letters. Twelve calls.

MISSIE. Wow!

TEDDY. And he didn't go on a single date.

LEON. That's not true. I went on one. But it didn't work out.

MISSIE. What do you mean?

LEON. It didn't work, I'm telling you.

TEDDY. Oh, they had a very nice time. Sheila told me all about it.

MISSIE. Sheila? That was her name?

TEDDY. Sheila and I get pedicures every Thursday. She heard it straight from Naomi.

Section II: A Minyan of Women 51

MISSIE. Naomi is who he went out with?

TEDDY. Naomi is Sheila's daughter-in-law.

MISSIE. Who'd Naomi hear it from?

TEDDY. Naomi? She heard it from—

LEON. THAT'S ENOUGH!

MISSIE. So? You had fun with your personal? You had what to talk about?

LEON. *She* had what to talk about. Oh, please. Chit-chat. Chit-chat. Chit-chat.

MISSIE. Chit-chat? What kind?

LEON. Kind? There's only one kind. That's the problem.

MISSIE. You didn't give her a chance, probably.

LEON. I'm sorry, but I wasn't interested in her Siamese kitten's inner-ear operation and how her hair was poofin' just right that day. Just right.

MISSIE. So? Does a woman have to be your special entertainment for the evening?

LEON. No.

MISSIE. A twenty-four hour TV channel?

LEON. No.

MISSIE. A side show?

LEON. No.

MISSIE. Then what? What do you expect a woman to be?

LEON. It depends.

MISSIE. On what?

LEON. On who she's startin' out to be before she tries trying to be something all around different than from what she started to be in the first place!!!

TEDDY *(hanging up the phone, which she has merely used as a cover the past few minutes)*. Leon, your sister says the boys are—

LEON *(quickly)*. Tell those kids if they don't wait until Hanukkah, I'm takin' those playset parts and makin' a doghouse for Mazel.

MISSIE *(pause)*. Ha! What a hoax! What a scam! This dating thing doesn't work. Pull my ad.

LEON. Ah, don't pull your ad. It's a good ad.

MISSIE. "Modest movie lover throws up in strange offices." What's the draw?

LEON. Hey, you're funny. You're scared—but funny.

MISSIE. Scared? Of what? Of some guy like you not calling me? Afraid of some guy who doesn't know how to dress himself? Don't you have a tie?

LEON. I got a tie. I just can't find it right now.

MISSIE. Well? Have you looked for it?

LEON. That's none of your business.

MISSIE. Well, at least button your jacket. You look like an unfolded flag.

LEON. Hey, don't take it out on me.

MISSIE. What?

LEON. You being afraid and all.

MISSIE. Afraid of what?!!!

LEON. You know.

MISSIE. WHAT? Some jerk with no tie trying to sell me a five-and-dime dream and break my heart? AND WHY AREN'T YOU WEARING A TIE?!!

LEON. I GOT A TIE! AND DON'T ASK IF I LOOKED IN THE REFRIGERATOR FOR IT, BECAUSE I ALREADY DID! AND I GOT EVERY RIGHT TO LOOK IN THE REFRIGERATOR! IT'S MY REFRIGERATOR! *(Silence. After a beat. TEDDY picks up a letter.)*

TEDDY. Boy, would you look at this?!!!

LEON. What, now?

Section II: A Minyan of Women

TEDDY. Moira Kendle is completely beside herself.

MISSIE. What's the matter with her?

TEDDY *(reading a letter)*. She's got a son. He's met a girl. The girl's moving to Israel and he knows that if he doesn't marry her, he's going to lose her forever.

LEON. Sounds like she's threatening him.

MISSIE. You're so cynical. Maybe he's gonna wake up and see that she's the best thing that ever happened to him. Maybe he's gonna threaten her.

LEON. See? See how two people can drive each other crazy?

TEDDY *(smiling)*. Yep.

LEON. I gotta catch a bus. And my hat is sittin' on top of my desk. *(He starts to leave.)*

TEDDY. Your *sister*, Leon. The *chairs*, Leon. The *flowers*, Leon...

LEON. I *hear* you, Leon—I mean, Teddy. I hear you. *(He takes a deep breath and turns to MISSIE.)* My sister's settin' an extra place for dinner.

MISSIE. An extra place?

LEON. In case I...was to bring someone.

MISSIE. You askin' me?

LEON. You want I should run your ad?

MISSIE. I asked you, first.

LEON. Wait here. I'll get my hat. *(He exits.)*

TEDDY *(looking at Abe's picture)*. Oh, Abe. I think Bermuda is a distinct possibility.

MISSIE. What're you gonna tell Moira?

TEDDY. Read next week's paper. *(Pause.)* So? You gonna run your ad?

MISSIE. I don't know. It's no way to meet a person.

(LEON reenters tying his tie, and looking dapper.)

LEON. Hey, look what I found.
MISSIE *(smiling at TEDDY)*. Nice tie. It goes good.
LEON. It was right under my hat, too. Ready to go?
MISSIE *(handing TEDDY her Gold Card)*. Run my ad—and charge it! *(As they start to leave, TEDDY runs the charge card through the register—and smiles.)*

END

IN SPITE OF EVERYTHING
by Hindi Brooks

CHARACTERS:

IMA: A 50-to 60-year-old woman.
KHANA: A 30-to 40-year-old woman.

SETTING: *An apartment in Ramat Gan, Israel. The first night of the Gulf War.*

AT RISE: *It's pitch black. We can't see KHANA, hidden in the armoire. An "all clear" air raid siren sounds. When it dies away, IMA, offstage, knocks repeatedly at the door, but doesn't get an answer.*

IMA *(offstage).* Khana? Are you there?... Open the door. It's over...Khana?... It's me, your mother... Are you there?... I'm coming in. *(Tries to open the door. It's locked. She jiggles it. It doesn't give.)* I have to break in, Khana. *(Pushes against the door, grunts with the effort.)* If I can... Oy. You'd better be there, I'm probably going to need a nurse.

(IMA almost falls in—a gas mask box draped over one shoulder—a very wilted bouquet of flowers in her hand. She looks about in the sliver of light through the door.)

IMA. Khana?... Are you all right?... I saw you come in before the raid. Where are you? *(She switches on the light.)*

KHANA. Turn off the light! *(Relieved, IMA puts her gas mask box on the table and turns off the light.)*

IMA. Didn't you hear the all clear? *(She crosses to the window and opens the drape—a street lamp illuminates the room, dimly.)* You can come out now. The raid is over.

KHANA. No, it's a trick.

IMA. Would they sound the all clear if it's a trick? Wouldn't the army know if it's a trick?

KHANA *(derisively)*. The army!

IMA. Khana, I can't talk to an armoire. Come out.

KHANA. Not yet.

IMA. Look what Dovid sent you.

KHANA. I'll look tomorrow.

IMA *(looking at the flowers with a shrug)*. By tomorrow, you won't want it. *(Turning on the light again.)* Khana, I'm turning on the light.

KHANA. No!

IMA. They're gone. They won't come back again tonight.

KHANA. They *always* come back.

IMA. If you stay in there until morning, you'll come out with a *hoiker* and look like Quasimodo, and Dovid will break the engagement.

KHANA. If I'm dead, he won't have to.

IMA *(empathizing, but trying to stay "up")*. If you don't want his present, I'll go down the hall and give it to Dalia.

(KHANA emerges from the armoire, taking off her gas mask.)

KHANA. You give his present to Dalia and *I'll* break the engagement. *(Looking at the flowers.)* She can have them.

IMA. I'm sorry they're wilted. Everyone was crowded together in the shelter, and that gorilla, Ari, kept breathing on them... Are you all right, Khana?

KHANA. Not until it's over.

IMA. It's over.

KHANA. The war.

IMA. Khanalah... *(She touches KHANA, KHANA moves away from her.)*

KHANA. Don't comfort me.

IMA *(puts the flowers on a chair and follows her)*. Let me hold you.

KHANA. Don't hold me. Stop holding me.

IMA. I love you.

KHANA. Don't love me either. I don't want to be loved.

IMA. Khanalah, it's not going to happen again.

KHANA. That's what you said. That's what you promised. And you lied.

IMA. I didn't say we wouldn't be attacked again. I said, no matter what they do, they won't destroy us.

KHANA. That doesn't sound like destruction to you?

IMA. We've heard worse.

KHANA. I'm sorry, Ima. Tell Dovid the engagement's off. *(Takes off her ring and puts it on the table.)* Tell him to go propose to Dalia.

IMA. He doesn't want Dalia. He wants you.

KHANA. I'm bad luck.

IMA. You *had* bad luck. How many years are you going to punish yourself for it?

KHANA. Not much longer. I'm an old woman.

IMA. And what does that make me?

KHANA. You'll never get old.

IMA. So what does that make you?

KHANA. The kiss of death. *(IMA takes her arm, propels her to the chairs, makes her sit down, and sits facing her.)*

IMA. Khanalah, Dovid is not Yehudah, and he's not Shlomo; he's not a soldier, and this is not the Six-Day War and it's not the Yom Kippur War, and he's not going to be killed. It's safe for you to love him.

KHANA. That's what I thought when I loved them. I won't do it a third time, Ima. I won't love someone again, and watch him die.

IMA. He's not going to die, Khanalah.

KHANA. How do you know? You'll probably be dead, too.

IMA. No, my family lives to a very old age.

KHANA. Except the ones in the concentration camps.

IMA. *I* escaped the camp. And I'll escape this, too. So will you. And so will Dovid.

KHANA. You made a pact with Hussein?

IMA. Sure. He promised not to kill us, and I promised, if I ever saw him, I'd blow him in a million pieces and sprinkle him over the gulf, on top of the oil.

KHANA. And the next day, someone else will start. And the day after that, another.

IMA. I love you, Khanalah.

KHANA *(gets up and moves away from her)*. No.

IMA. And Dovid loves you.

Section II: A Minyan of Women

KHANA. And I can't love anyone.

IMA. I'll teach you how.

KHANA. What are you, Ima? A masochist? You like getting your heart torn apart?

IMA. What can I do? I'm a romantic.

KHANA. That's romantic? You love someone, you make babies with him, and you lose him—*and* the babies—to the ovens?

IMA. But I *had* them. Like you had Yehudah and Shlomo.

KHANA. It would have been better if I didn't.

IMA. Then you would have had nothing.

KHANA. Then I would have had nothing to *lose*. You know how I exist now, Ima? When I'm not hiding from the bombs? I try to pretend I never was in love. I try to pretend there never was a Yehudah or a Shlomo.

IMA. And I exist by remembering when I had Yussel... and Hershel and little Golde.

KHANA. It's too painful to remember.

IMA. I remember making love to Yussel... and playing soccer with Hershel... *(With a reflective laugh.)* and Goldela trying to take the ball away from us.

KHANA *(IMA's getting to her).* ... Yehudah played soccer.

IMA. I remember.

KHANA. Shlomo was too busy with his books for such— No, I have to forget them!

IMA. If we forget them, we deny they existed.

KHANA. I'm not denying, Ima. I *do* think about them. Both. First one, then the other. I can't help it. But I can't do it like you do, Ima. I can't say, "Wasn't it nice I had them?" *(Feeling cornered, moving into a corner.)* Because I *don't* have them. Because every time, I have someone, they—he—they— *I* was in the army. Why didn't they kill *me*?

IMA. They knew we needed you. *(Going to her.)* Khanalah, I lost my family. Now, I have a new one. I have you. *(KHANA tries to get away from IMA but she blocks her during the following.)* When I saw you in the home...suddenly all the other motherless children... I stopped seeing them. I saw only you.

KHANA. They're not bombs, Abba said. They're firecrackers, to celebrate the new nation of Yisrael.

IMA. You were so thin. Your eyes were so— You didn't look 4 years old, you looked...maybe 2. I said, "I'll take that one."

KHANA *(remembering, painfully)*. And then there was a bomb. Right on their bedroom. Right on their bed.

IMA. "Don't you want to see her papers?" they asked, "Don't you want to know her history?" "I'll take her." I said.

KHANA. I couldn't see them. There was so much smoke. I felt my way to their bed. But it wasn't there. They weren't there.

IMA *(riding over that)*. Because from that moment, from the moment you put your arms out to me—before, even. I was your mother and you were my daughter.

KHANA. See? I lose everyone I love!

IMA. Not me.

KHANA. You should have picked someone else.

IMA. I don't want anyone else.

KHANA. And Dovid should pick someone else.

IMA. Dalia?

KHANA *(a beat, then a shrug)*. Let it be Dalia.

IMA. He doesn't love Dalia.

Section II: A Minyan of Women

KHANA. She's crazy about him.

IMA. She's crazy, period.

KHANA. And I'm the picture of sanity?

IMA. Well, you're crazy, too. But you're beautiful.

KHANA *(beginning to laugh)*. You're crazy.

IMA. But I'm beautiful. *(KHANA half-laughs, half-sobs.)* See? I made you laugh. *(She touches KHANA's face. KHANA pulls back, but not so forcefully now.)*

KHANA. I don't want to laugh.

IMA. What's better? To cry? *(KHANA's laugh is more a laugh now, and less a sob. IMA tries to embrace her. She pulls away.)*

KHANA. It's what I do best.

IMA *(teasing)*. That's not what Dovid says.

KHANA. No, not anymore. It's too late now.

IMA. It's almost morning.

KHANA. For babies. I can't have babies anymore, Ima.

IMA. Maybe you'll be lucky like me, and find the right one in the home.

KHANA. ...It's too late. Too many years—

IMA. You have many, many more. You want to use them up punishing yourself for...for your bad luck? You want to use them up punishing Dovid. And me? You want to punish someone, Khanalah? Punish *them*. *(IMA goes to the window.)* Let them know they're wasting their time with us. *(Calling out the window.)* We're not buying your message! *(Going back to KHANA.)* We have better things to do. *(KHANA has been taking it all in, beginning to believe. IMA takes the flowers.)* So do you want Dovid's ugly present or not?

KHANA *(hesitates, then takes the flowers)*. It's a beautiful present.

IMA. Maybe if I put them in water— *(IMA takes the flowers from her and puts the flowers in the vase. KHANA watches, then:)*
KHANA. Promise me you won't die, Ima.
IMA. I promise you I'll live to a hundred and twenty.
KHANA. And Dovid won't die.
IMA. He'll live even longer.
KHANA. Swear it.
IMA. On the memory of my family.
KHANA. Maybe I can love him.
IMA *(picks up the ring)*. In that case, he'll live forever. *(IMA tries to put the ring on KHANA's finger, but KHANA takes it from her.)*
KHANA. I want Dovid to put it on. Where is he?
IMA. Looking for the rabbi. To arrange for the wedding.
KHANA *(starting out)*. At the *shul*?
IMA. If there's still a *shul*.
KHANA *(coming back)*. You know why I love you?
IMA. Because I'm paying for the wedding?
KHANA *(laughs)*. Because I don't know what I'd do without you. *(They hug. Suddenly, the air-raid siren is heard. KHANA freezes. IMA gets their masks, gives one to her, and holds her closely. Still holding KHANA, IMA turns off the light. In pitch black, the siren continues for a moment, past the curtain.)*

END

THE GER (The Convert)
by Leslie B. Gold and Louis Greenstein

CHARACTERS:

SARAH: 30s
MOTHER: 50s
RABBI (may be live or taped as below)

Note: Offstage voices of the three rabbis have been produced with equal success as that of an onstage rabbi.

SETTING: *In blackout.*

SARAH. Whither thou goest I will go, and where thou lodge, I will lodge. Thy people shall be my people, and thy God my God...
RABBI. Are you sure you want to do this?
SARAH. Yes. I'm sure.

AT RISE: *Lights up on SARAH behind a free-standing curtain, covering her from shoulder to floor.*

RABBI. Suppose it's time to light the Shabbos candles, but your baby is in the bathtub. Do you leave the baby in the water so you don't miss Shabbos, or do you light candles later?
SARAH. I would take care of the baby. Laws of Shabbat can be suspended when there's a reasonable question of life and death. *And* I have until sunset to light.

RABBI. Name the major festivals.
SARAH. Sukkot, Shmini Atzeret, Pesach and Shavout...
RABBI. What is the meaning of Pesach?
SARAH. On Pesach we remember the Exodus from Egypt.
RABBI. And Shmini Atzeret?
SARAH. The eighth and ninth days of the solemn assembly; it's the end of Sukkot.
RABBI. Why eighth and ninth? Why do we observe two days of *yontuf* in the Diaspora while only one in Israel?
SARAH. Since we—I mean the Jews—go by the lunar calendar, the days of observance are based on the sighting of the new moon, which would be different from place to place. So with the Diaspora, and Jews being scattered all over the earth, if the festivals are on two days, all Jews are sure to celebrate at the same time. I read that in ancient times, bonfires were lit on hilltops in the land of Israel to signal to the people that the festivals were beginning. When people who were hostile to Jews started lighting their own bonfires as decoys, the Jews began sending messengers on foot to inform the people of the festivals. And since it often took these messengers more than one day to get to the distant communities, a second day was added.
RABBI. Good.
SARAH. Thank you.
RABBI. Why on earth do you want to do this?
SARAH *(beat)*. I think it's that my *neshama* has always been Jewish. It's always been in me. Something that was always meant to be.
RABBI. And your family. How does your family feel about this?
SARAH. My family...accepts my decision.

(Lights up on MOTHER. SARAH crosses to her and hands her a large carton.)

MOTHER. Thank you, honey. *(Looks into box and smiles perfunctorily.)* Oh. Pots and pans. How interesting.

SARAH. They're for *kashering* your kitchen, Mom.

MOTHER. I see.

SARAH. Mother. I will not get into this again.

MOTHER. There's nothing to get into. Obviously, my kitchen isn't clean enough for you. It's clean enough for your father and me.

SARAH. Mother, please don't. It's not about being clean. It's about choosing to live by different laws.

MOTHER. I see. You choose different laws, and then I'm supposed to turn my kitchen inside out.

SARAH. You said you wanted to support me in this. That you want me to be able to eat in your house.

MOTHER. Do you know who's dined in our home? Congressmen, executives, your Aunt Claudia, for heaven's sake!

SARAH. Mother!

MOTHER. Do you mean to tell me that this Jewish God doesn't want you eating your own mother's food?

SARAH. Not when it's a crown pork roast. *(A beat.)* Mother. Please. Don't take this personally. It's not about you. It's not about your kitchen. It's about me.

MOTHER. I don't understand, What's happening to you? *(Lights fade out on MOTHER. SARAH crosses to behind curtain.)*

RABBI. Are you sure you want to continue?

SARAH. Yes. I'm sure.

RABBI. What are the three *mitzvot* specific to women?

SARAH. Women are commanded to light the Shabbos candles; to take Challah; and to observe the laws of family purity.
RABBI. What work is forbidden during a festival?
SARAH. Any work that's forbidden on the Sabbath, except cooking from an existing flame and carrying.
RABBI. Where are we commanded to place a *mezuzah*?
SARAH. On every doorway of the house...except a door used only for deliveries and bathrooms.
RABBI. Very good. Now, in Exodus, Hashem commands us to honor our father and mother...

(Lights up on MOTHER. SARAH crosses to her.)

SARAH. Why are you so threatened by this?
MOTHER. I am not threatened!
SARAH. Then what is it?
MOTHER *(tentatively)*. I thought it was nice when you took that Jewish language class.
SARAH. Yiddish.
MOTHER. I loved when you read those wonderful stories to me. I was just as interested as you were in finding out about the Jewish people—their history, their customs. It's a lovely culture. But it's not *our* culture, dear.
SARAH. It's going to be mine, whether you like it or not. *(A beat.)* I'll ask you again, Mother. Please. Why do you feel threatened by this?
MOTHER. I suppose I'm afraid of losing you.
SARAH. What losing me? I'm right here, aren't I?
MOTHER. How can you think that they'll actually consider you one of them. What do they call it, *"guy-im"*? You think I haven't heard that word? That's what you'll be to them.

SARAH. Do you know that *goyim* only means "nations"? And anyone who uses it any differently is sadly mistaken. Mother, Jews are commanded to accept converts as no different from any other Jew. They're not even supposed to mention it.

MOTHER. Commanded! You're an outsider. You can never really be one of them.

SARAH. I've spent the last two years with these people. I've spent every Shabbos learning with a family in the Northeast*. I help cook Shabbos meals. We sit around till two in the morning singing, learning about Torah. Learning what it means to be a Jew.

MOTHER. Good Lord. And you don't feel out of place?

SARAH. I can't explain why, Mother. I don't understand it myself, but I feel more comfortable in a roomful of Jews than I do with Gentiles.

MOTHER. I suppose that includes *this* Gentile.

SARAH. You're my mother. You'll always be my mother. *(A beat.)* When I was little, I used to lie in bed at night, and I'd look up at the corner of the ceiling, and that's where God was. He was an Indian chief, just sitting up in my bedroom ceiling, in a full headdress, watching over me. Protecting me.

MOTHER. I remember.

SARAH. I'd talk to him— I'd tell him about school, ask him why Carol Bradley didn't invite me to her birthday party. And when Grandpa died, I asked him where he went. I used to fall asleep with God the Indian chief watching over me. I felt so safe. I don't know what happened, but he disappeared. I didn't notice for a long time. I never stopped believing,

* May substitute the name of a Jewish community in your area.

I just didn't spend any time thinking about it. I never talked to him anymore. I was too busy trying to find myself.

MOTHER *(ironically)*. I remember that too.

SARAH. I was looking for something. I didn't know what it was or where to find it, but I thought I sensed it one day when I was driving, I looked over at this tree, standing alone in a field, a beautiful weeping willow. It was so incredibly green. I stopped the car and just sat there. I could easily see the divinity in that tree, but I still couldn't see it in myself. Later on, when I went to the *ashram*, the meditation I learned helped me relax, but that was it. And as much as I didn't buy religion, I even tried a few churches, but they just didn't feel right. It wasn't a fit. Remember when I was in college and I made friends with that Jewish girl, Robin? We used to talk about spirituality all the time. I asked her tons of questions. She gave me books to read. The more I learned, the more questions I had. One Friday night, just out of curiosity, I asked her if I could go to services with her. Believe me, I never imagined I'd find my spirituality in Judaism, but when I walked into that room, for the first time since I was a little girl, I got the feeling that God was there, inside me, protecting me. And here was this roomful of strangers that felt like family. I knew I was in the right place. I knew I belonged. I remember the moment when it all came together for me—when I decided to convert. After years of learning and hanging around the community and struggling with every other option, Robin and I were in the middle of dinner and I just started crying. I asked her "How do I get in?" Mom, please accept this. I am finally happy. I want you to be part of my happiness.

Section II: A Minyan of Women

MOTHER. But you're not a Jew. You weren't raised a Jew.

SARAH. Don't you think I know that, Mother? You're right. I don't have my own Jewish history, or memories of my grandparents' Seder, or childhood memories of Chanukah. They say it takes three generations to make a Jew, to weave a history. But the more I practice my Judaism, the more I *daven*, the more I observe the *mitzvot*, every day that I take part in the rituals of being Jewish, the more I *feel* Jewish. And they tell me that your *neshama* actually changes when you go to the *mikveh*.

MOTHER. You'll never be one of them. You don't even look Jewish.

SARAH. Bigotry rears its ugly head.

MOTHER. That's not fair.

SARAH. Look at my face, Mother. Whether you like it or not, this is the face of a Jew. Now, will there be other Jews who have difficulty accepting me? I suppose there will be. And you know what? I'll feel sorry for them. And I'll know that their prejudice is just as unacceptable as yours.

MOTHER. Prejudice? No, not prejudice. Let me tell you about when I was a little girl and I'd lie in my bed at night. There was no God in my ceiling, no Indian chief. Just me, alone in my bed, shaking with fear that the Nazis were going to burst in and take me away. Never mind that we weren't Jewish and we lived in Bryn Mawr*. I was terrified! The Jews have been so...victimized! I've never had anything but respect, never anything but sympathy for these people. But they're a "them," they're not an "us." How can you want to be one of them? How can you want to be a member of a group that's been wronged

---
* May substitute the name of an affluent community in your area.

throughout its entire history? And how do you expect me to react when you're denying who you really are?

SARAH. I'm accepting who I really am. *(Blackout on MOTHER.)*

RABBI. Do you understand and accept all of the laws of Sinai and Torah?

SARAH. Yes, I do.

RABBI. Are you aware that you may be subjecting yourself to discrimination, hostility, possibly death?

SARAH. I am aware...

RABBI. That even in this day and age, here in America, the cradle of freedom, there are those who will want to kill you. Kill your children. Do you understand that?

SARAH. Yes.

RABBI. That though you may cry bitter tears, there is no going back. Once you're a Jew, you're always a Jew.

SARAH. Yes. I do.

RABBI. These people who have been hounded and persecuted throughout the centuries. You actually wish to become—of your own free will—one of us?

SARAH. Rabbi, you once told me that all Jewish souls were present at Sinai when the Torah was given. *All* Jewish souls—past, present and future. If I am to be a Jew, that must mean that my soul was there. I think my soul has waited long enough. I want to be a Jew.

RABBI. Sarah bas Avraham, you may immerse yourself in the water. *(A pause. Fading to black.)*

SARAH. Whither thou goest, I will go. *(We hear the sound of water.)* ...and where thou lodge, I will lodge. *(Water again.)* ...thy people shall be my people, and thy God my God... *(The last water. Blackout.)*

END

Section III:
White Spaces Black Letters

A GOLDEN OPPORTUNITY
by Julianne Bernstein

CHARACTERS:

PICA: An artist.
AARON: Brother of Moses.
CALF: The golden one, itself.

SETTING: *Inside a tent/artist's studio. Early morning. Six days after Moses has left to talk to God.*

AT RISE: *PICA sits by a covered statue trying to sleep. AARON enters. Tiptoeing, he takes a peek at the statue underneath the cloth. He is stunned. He tries to sneak out, but kicks over a tool, and wakes PICA.*

PICA *(waking up)*. Huh? What?
AARON. Nothing. Go back to sleep.
PICA. But the snake is God. God is the snake. I am holding it like a baby. It is a baby. I go to kiss it, and it's bloody tongue shoots out at me and blazes me with fire!
AARON. You were dreaming.
PICA. Where have you been, man? I sent for you when it was still dark out.
AARON. What's the rush? Close your eyes for a bit—you're obviously exhausted.
PICA. Please, Aaron, my blood is going to overflow and ooze out my body like sap from a tree; we must unveil it now.

AARON *(throwing him a small sack of gold coins)*. Here.

PICA *(counting out the coins)*. Aaron?

AARON. You will be presented with the other half at the unveiling. And, Pica, everyone will be there, too. Now, you don't want them to see you with those dark circles under your eyes and that crooked back, do you? Take your time. Rest. Eat. Wash. You will want to look your best.

PICA. My best is now. With the look of work on me. Man, what are you waiting for? I'm ready for the committee's approval. Bring them on. I'll serve wine.

AARON *(sighs)*. Make it water and take your time. Maybe you want to make some last-minute changes.

PICA. No! I have looked upon nothing but this statue for three full days. And if the statue was not finished—I would keep on working until either the life in me was drained from my body or until the job was done. But, Aaron, the job is done. Get the committee. Now.

AARON. I understand your zeal, but wait until the sun is high. Then the people will be able to see your statue shine. See it sparkle.

PICA. I have had it with you. Is it not what you ordered?

AARON. Not I, it was the committee—

PICA. The committee, then. You're afraid they will not like it.

AARON. No. That's just it. They will like it very much. It is exactly what they wanted.

PICA. Then what?

AARON. I am thinking of what Moses would say.

PICA. But he is not coming back.

AARON. I believe that he is.

PICA. You are alone in your thinking, Aaron.

Section III: White Spaces Black Letters

AARON. But if Moses came down that mountain and saw your statue—this idol of worship—think of it, Pica. Think of what Moses would say.

PICA. Moses is gone. He has not thought of us, why should I think of him? Get the committee, Aaron. Bring them now.

(AARON exits. PICA begins straightening up. The cloth slowly falls off the golden CALF which opens its eyes.)

CALF. As long as you're doing a little spring-cleaning, wipe your hand smudges off my rump.

PICA. HOLY COW!!!

CALF. And a howdy hello to you too.

PICA. What are you—*who* are you?

CALF. You don't know? What've you been doing for the last three days? Making fig newtons?

PICA. I did this?!

CALF. No. I appeared out of nowhere. Poof, poof, instant cow. Of course you did this. *(PICA starts praying desperately.)* Already you're worshipping me. Please. Let me wake up first.

PICA. I...didn't...expect...

CALF. What?

PICA. That you'd speak.

CALF. So? Arrest me.

PICA *(calling off)*. Aaron! Aaron! *(To CALF.)* Look at him. Zig-zagging his way across the camp. Moving as slowly as a— Hey! Yo! Aaron! *(Motioning for AARON to return. To CALF:)* Your name. Tell me. What is your name?

CALF. Give me one.

PICA. I...I...don't know.
CALF. You gave me life, but you can't think of a name? Get with the program, Pizono.
PICA. My name's not Pizono. It's Pica.
CALF. Then call me "Son of Pica" or "Pica Two." Hey, that's got a nice ring. Easy to chant. Pica Two, Pica Two, Pica Two, Pica Two...
PICA. Ah, finally. Here he comes. *(To CALF.)* Now. Get ready.

(CALF turns his head upstage as he was before. AARON enters.)

AARON. What is it? What's wrong?
PICA. I've...made this...discovery.
AARON. Something you want to fix? Fine. Go right ahead.
PICA. No. Not fix.
AARON. Then what?
PICA. To...celebrate.
AARON. Celebrate what, man?!! For the sake of my mother, and sister Miriam, be straight with me.
PICA *(looking at CALF)*. Tell him. *(PICA looks at AARON who is dumbfounded.)* Pica Two. *(CALF does not respond.)* Son of Pica. *(CALF remains frozen.)* Goldie. Buster. Cowpow. Chopsticks!
AARON. Pica?
PICA. We had a conversation.
AARON. Who, my friend?
PICA. The calf and me.
AARON. Another dream. You need rest, Pica.
PICA *(to CALF, desperately)*. Please. Say something.

Section III: White Spaces Black Letters 77

AARON. That does it. As much as I want to run away, myself, I am going to hurry these matters so that we get this unveiling over with as soon as possible, so that you can rest. Until I return with the committee—be still. *(He exits.)*

PICA *(shaking the "dream" out of his head)*. It cannot be. It cannot.

CALF *(turning its head toward PICA)*. As I was saying...

PICA. Oh, now you decide to speak.

CALF. I speak to no one except you, Big Daddy.

PICA. But I made you for *all* the people.

CALF. For them to worship, yeah. But nothing in my contract says I gotta talk to 'em. Besides, if I speak, they'll respond. It's all too complex.

PICA. Hey, I made you. You'll do what I say, you little heifer. *(Pause.)* You should be generous and spread your wisdom.

CALF. Wisdom, shmisdom! Do I look like I wanna work?

PICA. But you have to speak to them.

CALF. Hey, all I have to do is sit still, look pretty, while everyone dances around me. If they wanna treat me like I'm the Grand Chop, let 'em. No skin off my rear. *(After a beat, PICA unties the ropes around CALF's hooves.)* What are you doing?

PICA. Sending you away.

CALF. To where?

PICA. Anywhere. Roam back to Egypt if you want. I don't care. Just get out.

CALF. Is it something I said?

PICA. Ugh! I'm sick of you. Be gone! *(PICA starts pushing CALF.)*

CALF. But you can't send me away.

PICA *(pushing)*. I made you, I can send you away.

CALF. But I am the only thing of beauty you have ever created.

PICA *(stops pushing)*. That's not true.

CALF. Yeah? What other things have you made?

PICA. Bricks, seats of clay.

CALF. Things of beauty, I said.

PICA. Just go. Besides, you'd be unhappy as an idol of worship.

CALF. Are you kidding? It's a great job. No responsibilities except to keep up my dapper looks and play my part as the guest of honor.

PICA. Get out of my sight or I will carve out your tongue, melt it down and seal shut your mouth so that I cannot hear your stupid remarks when I send you away!

CALF. How can you send me away? You're responsible for me. *(Pause.)* It's your hands that have rubbed alongside my legs and neck these past three days. It's your delicate chisel that has made my ears lean and angular. It's your breath and strength of will that has made me honest, sharp-witted and sound. You made me for all to worship and for all to know as their new and improved God.

PICA. I will start from scratch, then. I will make another statue. And this time, I will put boils all over its face and give it the skin of a leper. I will make it so hideous, worshippers will want to smash it into thousands and thousands of pieces because the sight of it will make them sick.

CALF. Ha! God won't let you create something so gross and disgusting. He knows you're better than that.

Section III: White Spaces Black Letters 79

PICA. God's got nothing to do with it. These are *my* hands, *my* chisel, *my* sweat...

CALF. *My* this, *my* that. Who do you think is responsible for me turning out so beautiful in the first place? It wadn't no short-order cook. It was God. God gave you the talent, Pizono. And you better believe it.

PICA. There is no God!

CALF. Says who?!!

PICA *(pause)*. Moses said he would return after speaking with God. Well, Moses has *not* returned, leaving the people *without* a leader and *without* a God. I have a responsibility. If I can make them a statue of worship—I am answering to my responsibility as an artist.

CALF. But what of your responsibility as a Jew?

PICA. TALK TO ME NO MORE OF RESPONSIBILITY! Three days ago, I had finally finished a stool for the old woman next to my tent. I made it from this glorious red clay which hides beneath a thick bed of pebbles about two days walk from here. For many days, light and dark, I tore, rubbed, and chiseled until my hands were as red as the clay itself. I grew tired and felt as if I was back in Egypt making bricks and wanted to throw it all away, when suddenly—this stool, this throne—glistened like the jewels of the Pharaoh's daughter. So, with great pride, I presented it to the old woman who thanked me and sang all night about...how comfortable it was to sit on. How comfortable. Not a word of its beauty. Only of how useful and how...damned...comfortable. I wanted to take back the stool and hurl it against the rocks. I didn't care if the old woman sat on the bare ground the rest of her days, but I held my hand and tongue and ran with my rage to the other side of the camp and was drawing into the sand a face with tears when Aaron came along and looked at me with eyes that were tired and scared. "You have been chosen to create the Golden Calf," he said. *(Pause.)* I hid my joy and buried my face in Aaron's sandals so he would not see my tears and think me a child who was weak, but a man—an artist— that was strong and ready for responsibility. I looked up and saw Aaron's hand which he was holding out for me to take. I reached for it. I didn't know I was betraying him. God. The one God of Abraham, Isaac, and— *(Pause.)* But I took it. *(Silence.)*

CALF. You must destroy me.

PICA. But you are the only thing of beauty I have ever made. How can I destroy you.

CALF. How can you not?

(PICA picks up a large hammer and swings it back. AARON enters gasping for breath. CALF freezes. PICA gently puts down the hammer. AARON goes to an urn and drinks from it.)

AARON. Water, man. I need water.

PICA. Where's the committee?

AARON *(out of breath)*. I finally get them all together, we're maybe six tents away, and all of a sudden, Saul has to take a nap. He wants a nice soft bush to lay down next to. And then Mordi—he sees Rubin in the distance and remembers about some money he owes him, and then Old Ben starts shaking hands and telling stories like he wants to be king. So, Saul's snoring, Mordi's attacking Rub', and I'm completely losing sight of Ben because he's so short he's like lost in this crowd. But none of them matter because I got this band of angry worshippers coming right at me. They followed me here. They know I'm in charge.

PICA. Talk to them. Calm them.

AARON. As if I could stop a sandstorm from coming. They demand to see the calf. It's showtime!

PICA. But it's not ready.

AARON. What? Now you're not ready? Now you need time?

PICA. Do not take the calf.

AARON. What?

PICA. Don't give it to them.

AARON. What, then?

PICA. Give them your word that Moses will return.

AARON. Ha! My word is as good as this dumb animal's here.

PICA. Why can't you tell them to—

AARON. They will not listen to me.

PICA. But Moses said—

AARON. What Moses has said, they no longer believe.

PICA. They need a leader. Be their leader. Tell them to be patient and forgiving.

AARON. They are screaming for an idol to worship! One that they can see and touch. There is nothing I can say or do that will change that. Nothing! *(PICA swings back the hammer, about to smash CALF.)* Pica, no!

PICA. We don't have to see it ever again!

AARON. But you will have created it, Pica! You will always have created it! *(PICA lowers the hammer. AARON sighs.)* Why did I ever approach you in the first place?

PICA. You said I best suited the job.

AARON. Pica, I did not ask you because of your talent or your artistry. I asked you to make a fake and self-serving God—because I knew you would. *(AARON tosses him another sack of coins.)* The other half.
PICA. What?
AARON. Your payment.
PICA. I don't want it. *(He throws the sack of coins at AARON's feet.)* I don't want any of it.
AARON. I'll say you were too weary to attend the ceremony. *(AARON rolls out the CALF who opens its eyes for a moment before closing them and falling out of PICA's sight.)*
PICA. Too weary... Too weary... *(He picks up a sculpting tool, ready to begin work on something. He throws it down and begins to rub his hands in the sand. He grows more and more frantic, as if there is a stain on his hands that will never come off.)*

END

INTERVIEW WITH A SCAPEGOAT
by Louis Greenstein

CHARACTERS:

INTERVIEWER
GOAT

SETTING: *Azazel, a place cut off from the rest of us. The present.*

AT RISE: *We see GOAT limping along dejectedly. INTERVIEWER, carrying a backpack, enters, spots GOAT and immediately approaches it.*

INTERVIEWER. Say! Excuse me! Aren't you the scapegoat?
GOAT *(defensively)*. Who wants to know?
INTERVIEWER. Boy, am I glad I finally found you! I've been looking everywhere. I'm with the press. *(Flashes press credentials.)* You know, you are going to make one terrific story! *(Displays a small tape recorder.)* I see a book deal. I see a movie of the week. *(Turns on recorder.)*
GOAT *(looking about)*. I see a Godforsaken wilderness. No interviews! You got anything to eat?
INTERVIEWER *(searches through pockets and backpack, comes up empty)*. How do you feel?
GOAT. Guilty. I feel very guilty. And hungry as hell. *(Sighs; then suddenly becomes alarmed and skittish; re-*

gards INTERVIEWER suspiciously.) Say, you're not a high priest, are you?

INTERVIEWER. No. Just a reporter. *(Thrusts tape recorder into GOAT's face.)*

GOAT. Thanks. Don't mind if I do. *(Begins munching on the device. The INTERVIEWER is alarmed, wrestles the tape recorder away from GOAT and returns it to backpack.)*

INTERVIEWER. I can't believe you did that! I can't believe you tried to eat my tape recorder!

GOAT. You got a problem with that?

INTERVIEWER. Yeah. You eat like a pig!

GOAT. Obviously you've never fed a tape recorder to a pig.

INTERVIEWER *(testily)*. Look, I'm just doing my job, OK?!? I got a deadline! I don't need you to get testy...

GOAT. How typical.

INTERVIEWER. What do you mean?

GOAT. You shove something edible in the face of a hungry goat, right? The goat takes a bite. Why shouldn't he? He's a goat! He's doing his job! Your stuff's broken because you're an idiot. Ahh, and you blame the goat.

INTERVIEWER *(considers this and agrees)*. I never thought about it that way. I'm sorry. It's just that this is a plum assignment and I don't want to lose my job...

GOAT. Right. And naturally that's supposed to mean something to me. Oh, yeah. That's rich! I try and keep my nose clean, you people fling me off a cliff into the wilderness; I nearly break my neck, and now—help me out here, lemme see if I've got this right—somehow, I'm supposed to feel obligated to help you keep your job?

INTERVIEWER. But this would be good for you, too!

Section III: White Spaces Black Letters 85

GOAT. Right. It would further my career as a grazer. *(Wistfully.)* I had a job once.

INTERVIEWER. You still do. You bear iniquity. That's your job.

GOAT. Tell me something, would you? You applied for your job, right?

INTERVIEWER. Sure. Beat out eighteen other journalism majors.

GOAT. Well, I never asked to get flung off a cliff!

INTERVIEWER *(helplessly raising hands in the air)*. And I never suggested that anyone ought to fling you. But like it or not, flung goats are news. And you'd be pretty foolish to let a chance like this slip away.

GOAT *(sarcastically)*. Uh-huh. I see. How could I be so stupid, passing up on all those product endorsements, considering the marketing opportunities here in the barren wilderness. *(A beat.)* How'd you find me, anyway?

INTERVIEWER. Routine journalism. I hung around outside the tabernacle, asked a few questions, saw them slip you out the back door.

GOAT *(reciting from memory)*. "One for a burnt offering; and one for Azazel." What did I know? Sheesh, I thought I was lucky. Who'd have thunk? All this guilt to bear; and look at it out there. It's a wasteland.

INTERVIEWER. Why do they place all their guilt on you?

GOAT *(shrugs)*. Who knows? Tradition? Go ask the tribe.

INTERVIEWER. I'll get to them. But first, I want to hear the goat's side of the story. Tell me how it all started.

GOAT. It was a nice summer evening. I was in the manger, minding my own business, munching on an old tent stake, when all of a sudden, up walks this big, mean Levite. Son of a bitch attacks me and another goat and drags us to the tabernacle. I'll tell you something: sacrifice is work.

INTERVIEWER. What happened to the other goat?

GOAT *(slits own neck with finger)*. Burnt offering. Him, they roast. Me, they send on a guilt trip. Go figure. They blamed me for everything. One guy, I'll never forget, drinks too much wine at a sin offering, ducks behind the tabernacle to take a leak, trips over me, falls down and lands in his own puddle. Guess whose fault it is? He calls *me* a smelly animal and locks me in a cage for a week. They blamed me for all their problems. Oh, I got sick of it. Started doubting myself, even. And this goes on for quite a long time. *(Pause.)* Well, in goat years, anyway. One time, two boys get in a fight. Guess who got beat for it? It's the goat's fault since the boys watched me butt heads with a red heifer. How was I to know they were watching us? And who was watching them? Where were their parents? But hey, it's a lot easier to blame the goat than to raise your own children! Am I right?

INTERVIEWER. Good point.

GOAT *(looking around, sniffing and groaning)*. I'm hungry.

INTERVIEWER. Why are you so impatient?!? Now, I want my *story*! This is very important. I could lose my job if I don't get this story.

GOAT. No, you got it backwards. *I'm* important and *you're* impatient! I don't owe you a thing, but here you are ordering me around. You want something that I got. You're desperate. But you ain't gonna go around saying "what an impatient schmuck I am. How can I treat even a goat with such little respect?" No, no. You don't admit that to yourself. What do you do? You call me impatient.

INTERVIEWER. You know, I've taken about as much of your arrogance as I can handle.

GOAT. Me, arrogant? Yeah? And? What are you gonna do? Cast me out into the wilderness? Been there! Done that! *(Ponders for a moment.)* You know, people are right about one thing.

INTERVIEWER. What's that?

GOAT. The press is very, very cynical these days.

INTERVIEWER. Don't be ridiculous...

GOAT *(mimicking INTERVIEWER)*. "I see a book deal. I see a movie of the week. I gotta make my deadline or I'm gonna lose my job." Thank you, Walter Cronkite.

INTERVIEWER. That's completely unfair! Society's cynical. You can't blame the media for that. I'm just reporting what I see.

GOAT. Eh-eh. You're trying to make me into a sympathetic character so you can sell me. The problem is, I'm not sympathetic. I don't go down so easy. I'm not particularly nice. I'm mean. I'm selfish. Mostly, I'm hungry. *(A beat.)* Hmm, I wonder who'd play me in the movie?

INTERVIEWER *(ponders)*. Tell you what...

GOAT *(thinking aloud)*. Maybe George, from Seinfeld...

INTERVIEWER. You give me my story, "Interview with a Scapegoat," and I'll cut you in for twenty-five percent of all future profits, plus I'll feed you two notebooks. *(Pats backpack.)*

GOAT *(sniffing the pack)*. What else you got in there?

INTERVIEWER *(shooing GOAT away)*. Hey! Hey! Get outta there!

GOAT *(suddenly realizes something; approaches INTERVIEWER)*. You're afraid of me, aren't you? Holy cow. And I once knew a holy cow, incidentally. Son of Pica. Big ego. You're afraid of me. *(GOAT lunges at INTERVIEWER, but stops short of making physical contact.)* Grrrrrr!!! Ha-ha. Boo.

INTERVIEWER *(startled)*. AH! *(Trying to remain composed.)* Oh, come now.

GOAT. It's the same all over. You make me into some kind of beast, fling me off a cliff, banish me to a lousy neighborhood—I mean, would you look at this place. And I scare you.

INTERVIEWER. You seem angry.

GOAT. Angry? You're damn right I'm angry! You want my story? Fine! Here's what I've got to say. Write this down. *(INTERVIEWER complies.)* I'm a guilty goat. OK? Keeping a guilty goat around is how people manage to live with themselves. They screw around and call me oversexed. They butt in front of one another and stuff their faces and accuse me of eating everything in sight. They boast and they crow and spread gossip and lies behind each other's backs. And they have the nerve to call me filthy. *(GOAT pauses in reflection; INTERVIEWER scribbles notes; after a beat, GOAT continues.)* I think the whole business with the golden calf undermined their self-esteem. That's why they're so quick to lash out at idol worshippers. The truth is, we all have a bit of the idolater in us, don't we? We worship fashion. Personality. Wealth. Big cars. Then we wag our finger in the face of somebody else doing the exact same thing.

INTERVIEWER. So they project their guilt on you; they make you guilty. What a concept! What a story!

Section III: White Spaces Black Letters 89

GOAT. They point their finger at each other, too. *(Mimicking a conversation.)* "What do you do for a living?" "Well, I build bombs. And in my spare time I'm on a committee to stomp out street violence." The problem is: People don't know how to think. When they *think* they're thinking, they're not really thinking. They can't recognize that the only way to rise above their guilt is to rise above their behavior, not to stick it on somebody else.

INTERVIEWER. Does everyone do it?

GOAT. A kid from my mother's second litter knew a bullock who knew a pigeon who escaped from a big Hittite bash where they flung one goat off a cliff and roasted a second for a sweet savor unto some she-god.

INTERVIEWER. Must be written in their book, too.

GOAT *(shudders)*. That book. Don't remind me. It may be a guiding force for people. But when you're a goat or a ram it's pretty gruesome. Not so for swine, of course. Boy, I'd give my right hoof to be a pig.

INTERVIEWER. Ever read their laws?

GOAT. Nah, but I've heard 'em recited in the tabernacle enough times. And I once ate two cubits of parchment.

INTERVIEWER. I'm just trying to understand what the rules are about.

GOAT. God makes the rules. And God is big. You break one of God's rules and you feel like hell. But you still have to get up and go to work in the morning. You gotta go out there and put on a happy face. You gotta teach your children right from wrong without feeling like too much of a hypocrite. So what do you do about that nagging guilt you feel on account of the fact that you covet your neighbor's ass, or you snuck a BLT behind the marketplace? What do you do? You take your guilt and you stick it on something, somebody, some goat. You make them guilty! Like I said, everybody does it.

INTERVIEWER *(opens pack, removes two notebooks and hands them to GOAT, who immediately begins eating the paper).* Thanks. Listen, I gotta go. You've got quite a story. My editor will want to tweak it a little, I'm sure, but you give good quote. For a goat.

GOAT *(stuffing wads of paper in its mouth).* Frnk ru vwy mch. Mm. Vs zz gdd.

INTERVIEWER. Goodbye. *(Exits.)*

GOAT *(mouth still full of paper).* 'Rater. *(GOAT continues stripping paper from the books and eating luxuriously. Pauses. Scratches. Stretches.)* Baaahhhhhh!!!!! Baaahhhhh!!!!! Say, I wonder if there's any she-goats in this wilderness. *(Sings loudly.)* When I'm calling ewe, ewe, ewe...

(INTERVIEWER reenters.)

GOAT. You again?

INTERVIEWER. How do I get out of here?

GOAT. You're asking me?

INTERVIEWER. We're really cut off.

GOAT. No shit, Sherlock. How'd you find that out? Routine journalism?

INTERVIEWER. The rocks are slippery and the cliffs are awfully steep.

GOAT. This is Azazel. It's a place that's cut off. There's no getting out.

INTERVIEWER. But I wasn't sent here like you. I came on my own.

Section III: White Spaces Black Letters

GOAT. Then you're an idiot.

INTERVIEWER. No name-calling, you stupid-assed beast.

GOAT *(taunting)*. I'm rubber, you're glue. Everything you say bounces off of me and sticks to you!

INTERVIEWER. Shut up!

GOAT. Now *you're* mad.

INTERVIEWER *(angrily)*. AM NOT!

GOAT. Are too.

INTERVIEWER *(swings pack at the GOAT. GOAT ducks and INTERVIEWER falls down)*. You hurt me!

GOAT. Sure. I was trying to get out of your way.

INTERVIEWER. First you lure me here...

GOAT. You followed me, you dimwit! I got flung. You have no excuse!

INTERVIEWER. You insult me...

GOAT. You insult yourself.

INTERVIEWER. And now, you're becoming violent.

GOAT. Uh-oh.

INTERVIEWER *(lunges at GOAT)*. Ahhh! *(Chases GOAT, taking swings at it with hands, feet, and backpack. The GOAT evades the INTERVIEWER, seeming to enjoy itself. This riles INTERVIEWER, who steps up the chase and swings with more strength, even landing a few blows to GOAT. Finally, GOAT sticks out a foot and trips INTERVIEWER.)* Why, you... *(INTERVIEWER continues to chase, pummel, and kick GOAT.)* You nasty little bugger! How could you do this to me?! What did I ever do to you?! You're violent! You're mean! And you're totally out of control, you foul-mouthed little bastard!

GOAT *(scurrying around to evade the vengeful INTERVIEWER)*. Hey! Hey! Hey! Hey!

INTERVIEWER. Coward! Bully! Just wait'll I get my hands on you!

GOAT. Hey! Hey! Hey! *(Lights fade on the scene as IN-TERVIEWER chases GOAT around and around while notebook paper flies about and GOAT dives out of the way of INTERVIEWER.)*

END

About the Authors

Daniel Silberman Brenner *(Where's Your Stuff?)* is a reconstructionist rabbi and a senior teaching fellow at the National Jewish Center for Learning and Leadership (CLAL) in New York City. He began his training as a playwright in 1987 creating comedy sketches for the ARK Repertory Theater in Madison, Wis., and WORT-Wisconsin Public Radio. Since then he has written and performed comedy at small theaters and clubs in the United States, England and Israel. *Where's Your Stuff?* and *Meat* were professionally produced by Philadelphia's Theatre Ariel. His work was also featured at the National Museum of Jewish History in *Slavery to Freedom*, a piece Rabbi Brenner co-wrote as part of the Black-Jewish Artist Collective. He has written two full-length plays, *The Mystical Journey of Abraham Abulafia*, a drama about the 13th-century Jewish mystic and *Faster, Rabbi, Drill! Drill!*, a one-man comedy about spiritual leadership. Brenner lives in New York City with his wife Lisa and their sons Jonah and Noam.

Hindi Brooks *(In Spite of Everything)* writes for the stage, the page and television, teaches playwriting at UCLA and frequently lectures on writing. She has written numerous full-length and short plays, many of which have won awards. They have been translated into several different languages, produced internationally, and published. Her one-woman show, *Lily*, which deals with the Gulf War, tours internationally. She is a member of the Dramatists Guild, the Writers Guild, PEN, the Alliance of Los Angeles Playwrights, Theatre 40, West Coast Jewish Theatre and The Playwrights Group. She is listed in *Who's Who of American Film* and *Who's Who of American Women*. Brooks is married to actor Manny Kleinmuntz and is mother to actor Josh Kleinmuntz and writer-editor-photographer Nomi Isak.

Michael Elkin *(Class Act)* has won 19 national and regional writing awards and honors, including three fellowships from the Pennsylvania Council on the Arts—two for playwriting, one for screenwriting. He has had 11 plays produced across the country, including Los Angeles, Baltimore and Philadelphia. They include: *Cries in the Night* at the Walnut Street Theatre and *Fat Chance* at the Beverly Hills Playhouse. Elkin's work has been listed in *Plays of Jewish Interest* and *Best Plays of 1993*. Most recently, his play *Alex and Morris* was optioned off-Broadway and given a reading by the Jewish Repertory Theatre and Stageplays Theater. As entertainment editor of the *Jewish Exponent*, he has done more than 5,000 celebrity interviews. He is a member of the Dramatists Guild. Elkin dedicates this work to his beloved, late wife, Maxine.

Leslie B. Gold *(The Ger)* has spent most of her life in the theatre "backstage" as a stage manager, casting director, literary manager and producer for Ensemble Studio Theatre, The Vineyard Theatre, Theatre for the New City, and The American Jewish Theatre in New York, and in public relations and marketing at the Walnut Street Theatre in Philadelphia. At the Walnut, she moved "onstage" as an actor in Theatre Ariel's *Teible and Her Demon* (Genendel). Gold also appeared in Theatre Ariel's first *10x10*—as Sarah in Michael Elkin's *Class Act*, and as the lively corpse in Julianne Bernstein's *'Til Death Do Us Plots*. As an actor, Gold studied at the American Conservatory Theatre in San Francisco and the Groundlings in Los Angeles, but she found what she'd been searching for in her own backyard by studying Judaism with Aish Ha Torah in Los Angeles, then at She'arim College of Jewish Studies for Women in Jerusalem. Gold divides her time between her studies in Israel and teaching drama and playwriting while presently developing *Out of My Head*, a new one-woman show.

Vivian Green *(The Foot Peddler)* has had plays produced around the Delaware Valley, off-off-Broadway, and on NPR and WBAI radio. Her plays include *The Pact, In Loco Parentis, Dancing in the Dark, Single...Again, Westerbork* (commissioned by Theatre Ariel) and *Union Square* (finalist, Dorothy Silver Playwriting Competition). Her travel articles have appeared in national publications, and she has led numerous writing workshops. Her awards include a 1998 fellowship in theater from the Pennsylvania Council on the Arts, administered by the Theatre Association of Pennsylvania (TAP); an earlier TAP fellowship; and a Pennsylvania Humanities Council grant. Green is a member of the Dramatists Guild and TAP.

Louis Greenstein *(Interview with a Scapegoat, Smoke, The Ger)* is the author of more than 10 plays, including *With Albert Einstein* (co-written with Don Auspitz), *In the Wee Hours* and *The Rose of Contention*. Greenstein has been a recipient of a Pennsylvania Council of the Arts playwriting fellowship, and has been commissioned to write plays for Stageworks Touring Company and Theatre Ariel. His articles and essays have appeared in many national publications; he has worked as a freelance boxing correspondent; and has written for the Emmy Award-winning Nickelodeon series, *Rugrats*. Greenstein lives in suburban Philadelphia with his wife Catherine and their three children, Barry, Hannah and Sam.